Level Up with Azure AI Foundry

Understanding Innovative AI Development on Azure

Sagar Lad

Level Up with Azure AI Foundry: Understanding Innovative AI Development on Azure

Sagar Lad
Navsari, Gujarat, India

ISBN-13 (pbk): 979-8-8688-1867-7 ISBN-13 (electronic): 979-8-8688-1868-4
https://doi.org/10.1007/979-8-8688-1868-4

Copyright © 2025 by Sagar Lad

This work is subject to copyright. All rights are reserved by the Publisher, whether the whole or part of the material is concerned, specifically the rights of translation, reprinting, reuse of illustrations, recitation, broadcasting, reproduction on microfilms or in any other physical way, and transmission or information storage and retrieval, electronic adaptation, computer software, or by similar or dissimilar methodology now known or hereafter developed.

Trademarked names, logos, and images may appear in this book. Rather than use a trademark symbol with every occurrence of a trademarked name, logo, or image we use the names, logos, and images only in an editorial fashion and to the benefit of the trademark owner, with no intention of infringement of the trademark.

The use in this publication of trade names, trademarks, service marks, and similar terms, even if they are not identified as such, is not to be taken as an expression of opinion as to whether or not they are subject to proprietary rights.

While the advice and information in this book are believed to be true and accurate at the date of publication, neither the authors nor the editors nor the publisher can accept any legal responsibility for any errors or omissions that may be made. The publisher makes no warranty, express or implied, with respect to the material contained herein.

> Managing Director, Apress Media LLC: Welmoed Spahr
> Acquisitions Editor: Smriti Srivastava
> Coordinating Editor: Jessica Vakili

Cover image by Pixabay.com

Distributed to the book trade worldwide by Springer Science+Business Media New York, 1 New York Plaza, New York, NY 10004. Phone 1-800-SPRINGER, fax (201) 348-4505, e-mail orders-ny@springer-sbm.com, or visit www.springeronline.com. Apress Media, LLC is a Delaware LLC and the sole member (owner) is Springer Science + Business Media Finance Inc (SSBM Finance Inc). SSBM Finance Inc is a **Delaware** corporation.

For information on translations, please e-mail booktranslations@springernature.com; for reprint, paperback, or audio rights, please e-mail bookpermissions@springernature.com.

Apress titles may be purchased in bulk for academic, corporate, or promotional use. eBook versions and licenses are also available for most titles. For more information, reference our Print and eBook Bulk Sales web page at http://www.apress.com/bulk-sales.

Any source code or other supplementary material referenced by the author in this book is available to readers on GitHub (https://github.com/Apress). For more detailed information, please visit https://www.apress.com/gp/services/source-code.

If disposing of this product, please recycle the paper

મા કદાપિ ત્યજ

Never give up.

With deep gratitude, I dedicate this book to ચીખલી તાલુકા પ્રજાપતિ વિદ્યાર્થી આશ્રમ, *especially* **Chetan Lad (Choice Travels)** *and* **Dipak Lad**, *for their unwavering support.*

My heartfelt thanks to **Brijeshbhai/ Nikitaben Gajera, Abhishekbhai/ Mihikaben Shroff, Dwij, Nirvi,** *and* **Swanay**. *Thank you for creating the space that helped me bring this book to life.*

Table of Contents

About the Author ix

About the Technical Reviewer xi

Introduction xiii

Chapter 1: Getting Started with Azure AI Foundry 1

    The Fundamentals of Generative AI 2

    The Art of Prompt Engineering 8

    Introduction and Key Features of Azure AI Foundry 9

    Understanding the Azure AI Foundry Architecture 13

        Azure OpenAI 14

        Management Center 15

        Azure AI Foundry Hub 17

        Azure AI Foundry Project 19

        Connections 20

    Conclusion 22

Chapter 2: Exploring Azure AI Foundry 23

    Setting up Your AI Environment 24

    Connecting Azure OpenAI to AI Foundry Hub 32

        Use Azure OpenAI Outside an Azure AI Foundry Project 33

        Use/Connect Azure OpenAI Inside Azure AI Foundry 34

TABLE OF CONTENTS

Exploring Model Catalogs, Benchmarking, and Deployment...............36
    Model Catalogs..36
    Model Benchmarking 41
    Deployment 43
Chat Playground..44
Understanding Prompt Catalogs 51
Conclusion 57

Chapter 3: Building with Prompt Flow 59

Introduction to Prompt Flows......................................60
Creating Simple I/O Flows in AI Foundry........................62
Understanding the Copilot Stack..................................71
Web Classification Using Prompt Flow 74
    Define a Connection 74
    Develop a Prompt Flow..77
    Start a Compute Session 78
    Set up LLM Nodes 79
    Once the Prompt Flow Is Ready.............................80
Integrating External APIs with AI Foundry......................83
Function Calling and Advanced Workflows 86
Conclusion 88

Chapter 4: Bringing Your Own Data to AI Foundry............89

Introduction to Retrieval-Augmented Generation 90
Setting up a RAG Infrastructure and Prompt Flows 94
    Step 1: Set up RAG Infrastructure in AI Foundry...........97
    Step 2: Using a Prompt Flow with RAG......................99
Connecting and Managing Data Stores for LLMs............102
Conclusion 105

TABLE OF CONTENTS

Chapter 5: Exploring Multimodal AI Capabilities 107
AI Portfolio..108
    Key Features of Azure Speech Studio..110
Azure AI Vision's Capabilities 117
Using Azure AI Document Intelligence with Prompt Flows 122
    Step 1: Set up Azure AI Document Intelligence 122
    Step 2: Upload Sample Invoices 123
    Step 3: Test Document Intelligence in AI Foundry 125
    Step 4: Create a Prompt Flow..126
    Step 5: Design a Prompt..127
    Step 6: Run the Flow 128
    Step 7: Deployment 128
Protecting Sensitive Information with PII Detection...........................128
Conclusion 131

Chapter 6: Deploying, Monitoring, and Ensuring AI Safety...............133
Deploying and Debugging Prompt Flows 134
Integrating AI Foundry with Copilot..145
Monitoring and Managing AI Endpoints 153
Security, Governance, and AI Trustworthiness 156
Conclusion 163

Index..165

About the Author

Sagar Lad is a seasoned data solution architect with deep expertise in cloud, data, and AI technologies. With over a decade of experience working with leading global enterprises, including top financial institutions, Sagar is known for architecting innovative, scalable, and secure solutions on Microsoft Azure. He collaborates closely with product vendors like Microsoft and Databricks to identify fit-for-purpose tools and align solutions with enterprise architecture standards.

Based in the Netherlands, Sagar is a thought leader in data strategy, data governance, cloud-native analytics, and responsible AI. He has authored numerous articles across platforms like Medium, C# Corner, and Amazon, and frequently speaks on topics ranging from data mesh to AI ethics. Passionate about knowledge sharing, Sagar mentors aspiring architects and consults with organizations to turn data into business value.

Beyond his technical acumen, Sagar is committed to demystifying complex concepts and helping professionals *ladder up* their careers in the digital era. His writing blends practical insights with strategic thinking, making it an essential read for technology leaders and curious minds alike.

Sagar's LinkedIn profile is at `https://linkedin.com/in/ladsagar`. You can learn more about his professional certifications at `www.youracclaim.com/users/sagar-lad/badges`.

About the Technical Reviewer

Lakshit specializes in building and scaling product advocacy programs at startups and enterprises. He is a lead developer in community initiatives at Microsoft and has built dev communities for companies such as Meta, Intel, and Adobe, consistently delivering high-impact engagement strategies. His expertise spans developer ecosystems across Microsoft Azure, XR, GitHub Copilot, and the Microsoft Agentic stack.

Introduction

Welcome to your journey into the world of Azure AI Foundry. *Level up with Azure AI Foundry* is your practical guide to building and deploying cutting-edge AI solutions using Microsoft's Azure AI platform. Whether you're a data professional looking to deepen your AI skills, a cloud architect exploring generative AI capabilities, or a developer eager to build intelligent applications, this book is designed for you.

Why This Book?

Generative AI is revolutionizing how we work, create, and solve problems. Microsoft's **Azure AI Foundry** provides a powerful, end-to-end environment for building, evaluating, and deploying AI-powered applications at scale. However, navigating these tools and best practices can be overwhelming without structured guidance. That's where this book comes in.

With a focus on clarity, hands-on examples, and real-world use cases, *Level up with Azure AI Foundry* helps you confidently unlock the potential of Azure's generative and multimodal AI services—without drowning in buzzwords or unnecessary complexity.

Who Is This Book For?

- **Data engineers and solution architects** who want to build scalable AI workflows on Azure
- **AI/ML enthusiasts** eager to learn how Microsoft's AI tools can simplify model building, prompt engineering, and deployment

INTRODUCTION

- **Developers and analysts** exploring how to integrate language and vision models into real applications
- **Students and tech professionals** seeking a concise but complete understanding of Azure AI Studio and Foundry

What's Inside?

The book is structured into six focused chapters that progressively build your skills.

- Chapter 1 explains the foundational concepts of Azure AI Foundry and how it fits into the larger AI ecosystem. Set up your environment and get familiar with the tools and user interface.

- Chapter 2 dives into the features of AI Studio—explore model catalogs, prompt testing, chat playgrounds, safety settings, and key components of the AI Foundry ecosystem.

- Chapter 3 analyzes and implements Microsoft prompt flows. You learn to build I/O flows, chain multiple LLM calls, use external APIs, and integrate function calling within your flows.

- Chapter 4 helps you discover how to enrich your AI applications by integrating your own datasets using retrieval-augmented generation and Azure data indexing tools.

- Chapter 5 works with vision, speech, and document intelligence services to unlock multimodal use cases. You learn about building solutions that see, hear, and understand documents with Azure's AI capabilities.

- Chapter 6 demonstrates how to deploy your AI solutions responsibly. Topics include monitoring performance, implementing safety measures, and ensuring compliance with responsible AI principles.

Let's level up.

CHAPTER 1

Getting Started with Azure AI Foundry

Generative artificial intelligence, also known as generative AI or GenAI, is transforming the way you work, innovate, and interact with technology. From automating tasks to generating creative insights, its impact is undeniable. But to truly harness its power, you need the right tools and techniques.

In this chapter, you'll start by exploring the fundamentals of generative AI—how these models learn, think, and create. Then, you'll dive into the art of prompt engineering, the key to getting precise and useful responses from AI. A well-crafted prompt can make the difference between generic output and a game-changing insight. Next, you'll introduce Azure AI Foundry, Microsoft's all-in-one platform that simplifies AI development and deployment. You'll discover its key features and how it enables businesses and developers to easily build intelligent applications. Finally, you'll take a deeper look at the Azure AI Foundry architecture, learning the components that power this cutting-edge AI ecosystem.

Mastering these concepts is the first step toward building smarter, more efficient AI-driven applications. Let's get started.

This chapter covers the following topics.

- The fundamentals of generative AI
- The art of prompt engineering

CHAPTER 1   GETTING STARTED WITH AZURE AI FOUNDRY

- An introduction to Azure AI Foundry
- Understanding the Azure AI Foundry architecture

The Fundamentals of Generative AI

Imagine a world where machines don't just follow instructions but create—a world where AI can write stories, generate artwork, compose music, and even build software. This isn't science fiction; it's the reality of generative AI.

At its core, generative AI is a type of artificial intelligence that learns from vast amounts of data and generates new content that feels authentic and human-like. Think of it as an artist who studies thousands of paintings and then creates a masterpiece of their own—or a chef who tastes hundreds of dishes and then invents a new recipe. The term *generative AI* can be described as follows.

Artificial intelligence has existed for many years. Google Maps' estimating when you will reach a destination or Tesla's self-driving cars are examples of conventional AI. On the other hand, generative AI goes one level above, and it can generate content in the form of text, images, videos, or audio.

Consider an example of how ChatGPT uses generative AI to answer when writing a short email about congratulating a colleague on getting a promotion, as shown in Figure 1-1.

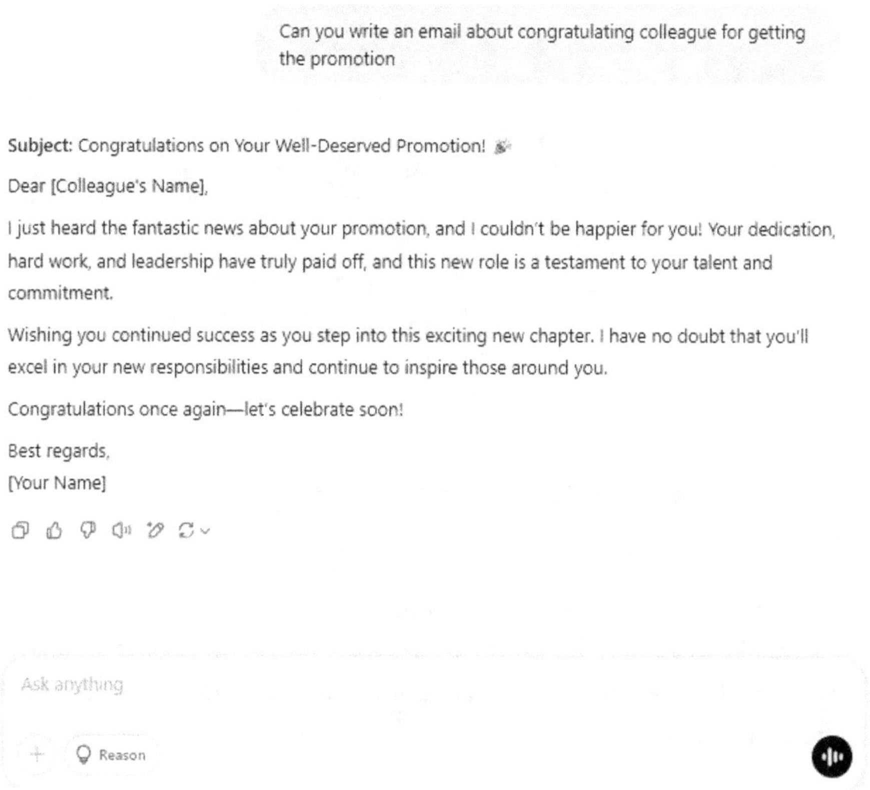

CHAPTER 1　GETTING STARTED WITH AZURE AI FOUNDRY

Figure 1-1. ChatGPT to write an email

Generative AI is an expansion of artificial intelligence that can generate new content in the form of text, images, video, audio, or code. Traditional AI mainly focuses on classifying data, making predictions about data, or understanding data sentiment, but generative AI creates new content. Figure 1-2 shows how data science, machine learning, deep learning, and generative AI are related.

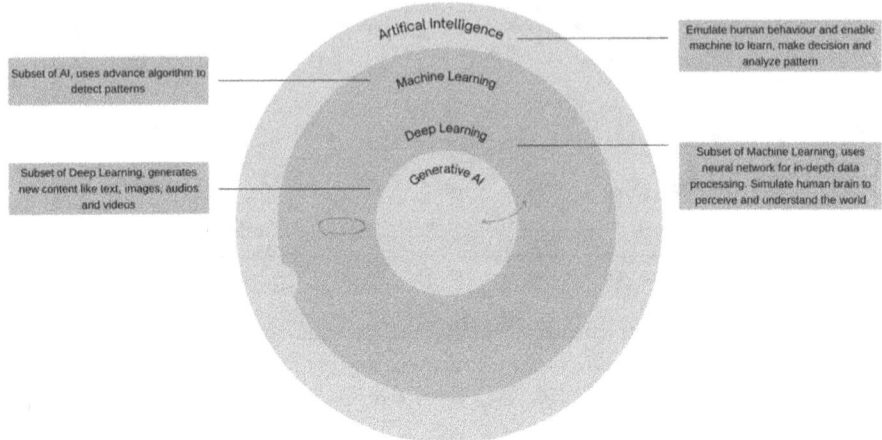

Figure 1-2. *Overview of AI, machine learning, deep learning, and GenAI*

Table 1-1 concisely compares AI, machine learning, deep learning, and generative AI, outlining their basics, use cases, and examples. It highlights how each technology contributes to various fields like automation, content creation, and data analysis.

Table 1-1. *AI Technologies and Use Cases*

Technology	Definition	Use Cases	Examples
Artificial Intelligence (AI)	Simulates human intelligence, decision-making, and problem-solving	Virtual assistants, chatbots, and autonomous systems	Siri, Alex, Google Assistant
Machine Learning	A subset of AI that uses data and algorithms to mimic human learning	Predictive analytics, spam detection, fraud detection	Recommendation systems in Amazon/Netflix
Deep Learning	A type of machine learning that uses neural networks with many layers to analyze large datasets	Image recognition, speech recognition, NLP	Self-driving cars, facial recognition
Generative AI	Uses models to generate new data based on learned patterns from existing data	Content creation, art generation, code generation	GPT models (ChatGPT), DALL·E

Let's now briefly examine some key aspects of generative AI.

- **Large language models (LLMs)**: LLMs are powerful intelligent models designed for generating human-like text (see Figure 1-3). People normally use generative AI and LLM terms interchangeably, but there is a thin difference. Generative AI can generate text, images, audio, video, and so forth, while LLMs can only generate text.

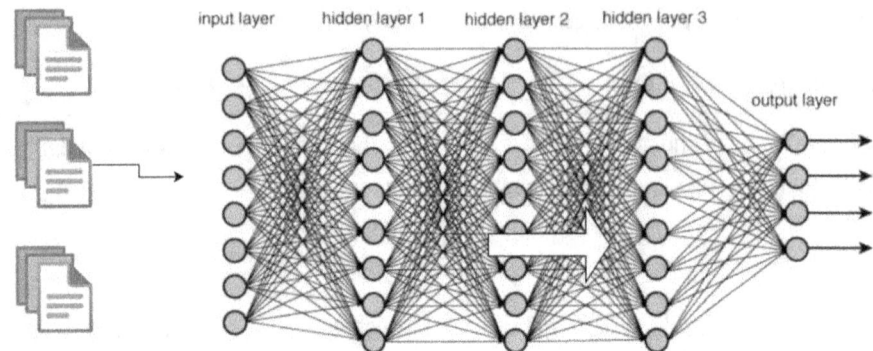

Figure 1-3. The workings of LLM

LLMs are trained on a large volume of publicly available data. As shown in Figure 1-3, the brain behind the large language model is like a human brain, called a neural network. In generative AI, you power these neural networks with transformers to produce better output. Transformers can understand language context like humans but process one word at a time.

- **Prompt engineering**: A prompt is a specific question, instruction, or input for the AI systems to receive a specific response or information. As shown in Figure 1-4, when you use the Alexa voice assistant, you give prompts to get the answers or to execute any action from Alexa.

Figure 1-4. *Amazon Alexa voice assistant prompts*

Prompt engineering is a process of creating well-defined and structured inputs to communicate with the AI systems to receive accurate and relevant responses. This is discussed in more detail in the next section.

- **Embeddings**: Embedding is a key component of generative AI. Machines don't understand text; only numbers. Embeddings are numerical representations of the text/prompt to understand the human language effectively. For example, give a prompt like, "I love cars." Embedding converts such statements into the vector representation of the number so the machine can understand.

- **Fine-tuning**: LLMs are pre-trained on the publicly available data. But if you want to use LLMs to get the work done per your/company's needs, you need to fine-tune them.

CHAPTER 1　GETTING STARTED WITH AZURE AI FOUNDRY

The Art of Prompt Engineering

Prompt engineering is a process of defining questions/input to the generative AI tools to generate content based on the task or take some action. You can define the prompt using natural language. Let's look at key considerations for defining a prompt.

- Express your input/query clearly and concisely.
- Give detailed background information.
- Create a prompt that is simple to understand.
- Perform iterative testing and refinement of the prompt.
- Follow up with instructions/questions.
- Use different prompting techniques.

The following describes the different types of prompting techniques.

- **Zero-shot prompting**: This is the simplest and most direct method of prompt engineering, where you give instructions to the generative AI without providing any background or additional information. This technique is mostly suitable for simple tasks rather than complex tasks.

- **Few-shot prompting**: In this type of prompting method, you must provide examples of the prompt to get an accurate output. It is more suitable for doing complex tasks compared to zero-shot prompting.

- **Chain-of-thought (CoT) prompting**: This method is more accurate because it breaks down complex tasks into small intermediate steps, which in turn helps generative AI models/tools produce more accurate results.

- **Prompt chaining**: In this prompting technique, a complex task is divided into multiple subtasks. Then, for each subtask, generative AI is used to produce the output and accomplish the overarching task. It is a more reliable method to get a consistent and accurate output.

Introduction and Key Features of Azure AI Foundry

Generative AI boosts productivity by automating repetitive tasks, generating high-quality content, and providing real-time insights. Companies leverage AI for faster decision-making, enhanced customer interactions, and streamlined operations, reducing costs and improving efficiency. There has also been a rapid advancement in GenAI technologies. To quickly adapt to these advancements and make the generative AI solution better, it is better to customize it. However, building the generative AI application is not very simple, but it is also a little difficult. You need to figure out which model to use, which AI service to use, orchestration, deployment, and monitoring.

Azure AI Foundry is a platform to develop production-ready, enterprise-grade AI tools like co-pilots, applications, and solutions. Azure AI Foundry is a composition of two components.

- **A collection of AI models and services**: You can discover the Azure AI models using the Azure AI Foundry model catalog without a project. From the Azure AI Foundry home page, select **Model catalog and benchmarks.** In the Collections drop-down menu, select **Microsoft**, search for "Azure AI services", and select the model to check for more information (see Figure 1-5).

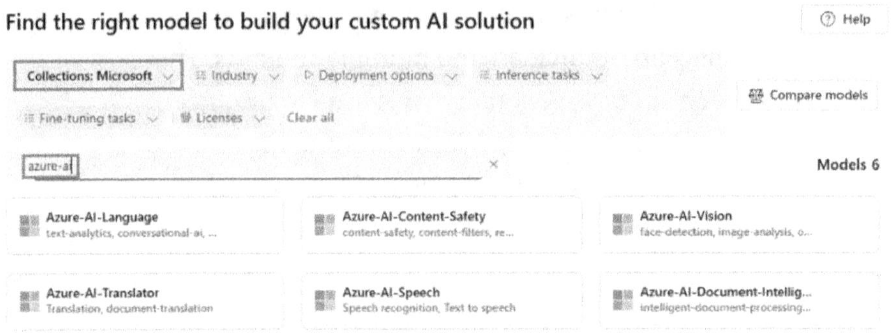

CHAPTER 1 GETTING STARTED WITH AZURE AI FOUNDRY

Figure 1-5. AI Foundry model catalog

- **A platform to build AI tools**: Azure AI Foundry is also a platform for building AI tools. You can use a no-code or low-code approach or a fully coded approach.

Azure AI Foundry is a one-stop shop for all the AI models and services to develop generative tools. Figure 1-6 shows it has a range of Azure AI services. If you need a model that can convert text to speech or speech to text, then you can use the Azure AI Speech service, or if you need a model that can take a picture of the receipt and transcribe and convert it to text, then you can use Azure Document Intelligence.

Figure 1-6. Azure AI services

CHAPTER 1   GETTING STARTED WITH AZURE AI FOUNDRY

Azure AI Foundry has a complete AI tool chain. You can use these tools to make your LLM context-aware with the data you provide (i.e., PDF, Word, text, or PowerPoint files, etc.). Search functionalities and functions within your large language model is also possible.

As you can see in Figure 1-7, with Azure Foundry, you can not only use Azure AI but also speech analytics, language translator, content safety, and other resources to build multimodal applications. Multimodal generative AI applications are very complex to build. For example, you want to build a ChatGPT-like system that uses the GPT model in the backend, but it takes input in the form of speech. With Azure AI Speech, you can convert user speech input into text, which can be given as an input to the GPT engine, which generates the result and gives it back to the user.

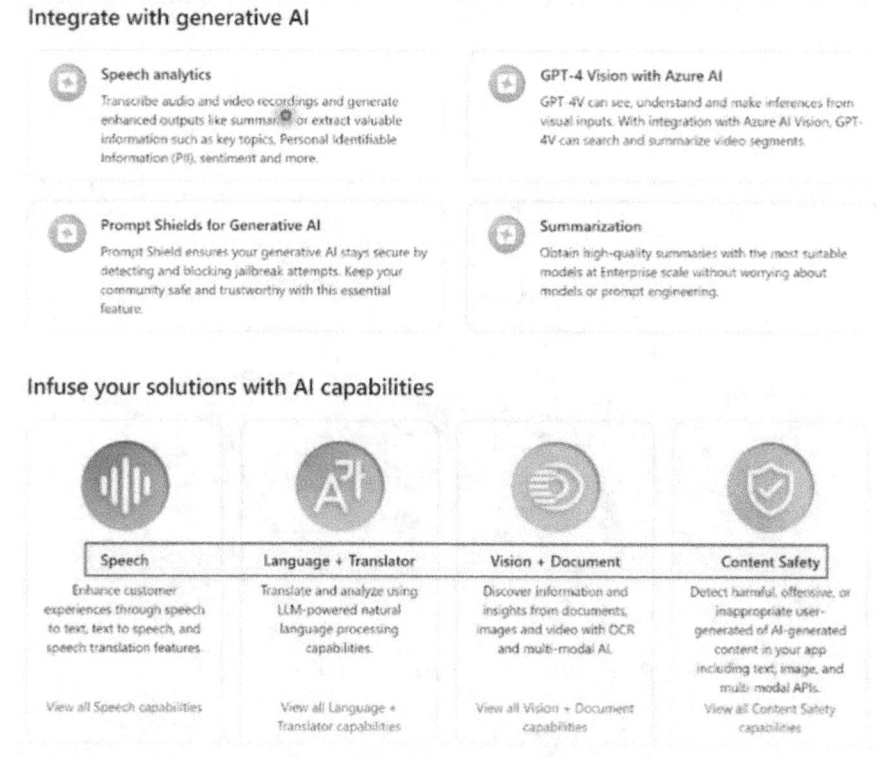

Figure 1-7. *Build multimodal GenAI applications*

11

Azure AI Foundry provides a unified experience and governance for all the Azure AI services and resources deployed in the Azure portal. It also has model benchmark features to select the best model by comparing the available models with various parameters.

Azure AI Foundry is a separate resource. It doesn't come when you deploy an Azure OpenAI instance. You must go to the Azure portal and deploy the Azure AI Foundry as a separate resource. Figure 1-8 shows that Azure AI Foundry has an AI hub with AI projects inside it. An Azure AI hub consists of shared Azure connections, which provide a unified governance experience as they are shared and not project-specific. These shared Azure connections can be for Azure Cosmos DB or Azure AI Speech, which anyone in the project can use. But if you want to create project-specific connections, you can create project-specific Azure connections that are not shared.

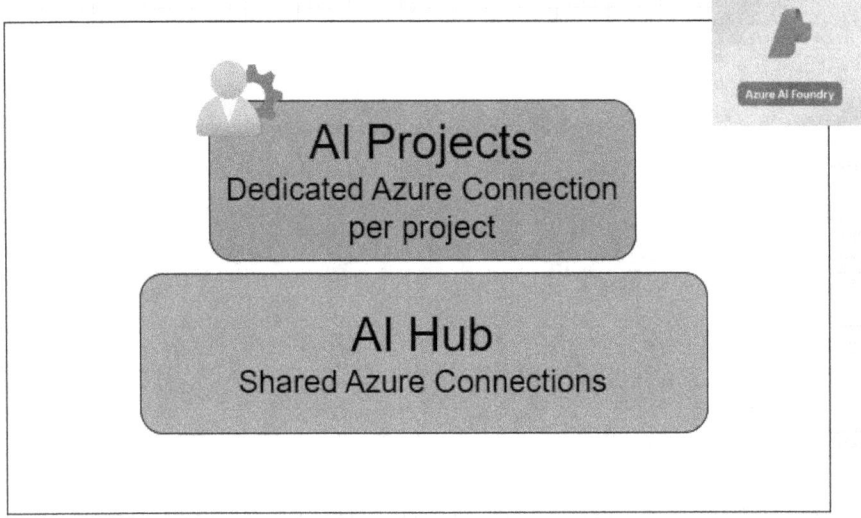

Figure 1-8. *Azure AI Foundry hierarchy*

CHAPTER 1 GETTING STARTED WITH AZURE AI FOUNDRY

So Azure AI Foundry provides a collaborative environment where developers can collaborate. But, if you want specific users to access specific projects and connections, it is also possible to implement it.

Understanding the Azure AI Foundry Architecture

Azure AI Foundry provides a unified experience for GenAI developers and data scientists to build, validate, and deploy AI models using the portal, SDK, APIs, or Azure CLI. Let's look at the Azure AI Foundry architecture in more detail (see Figure 1-9).

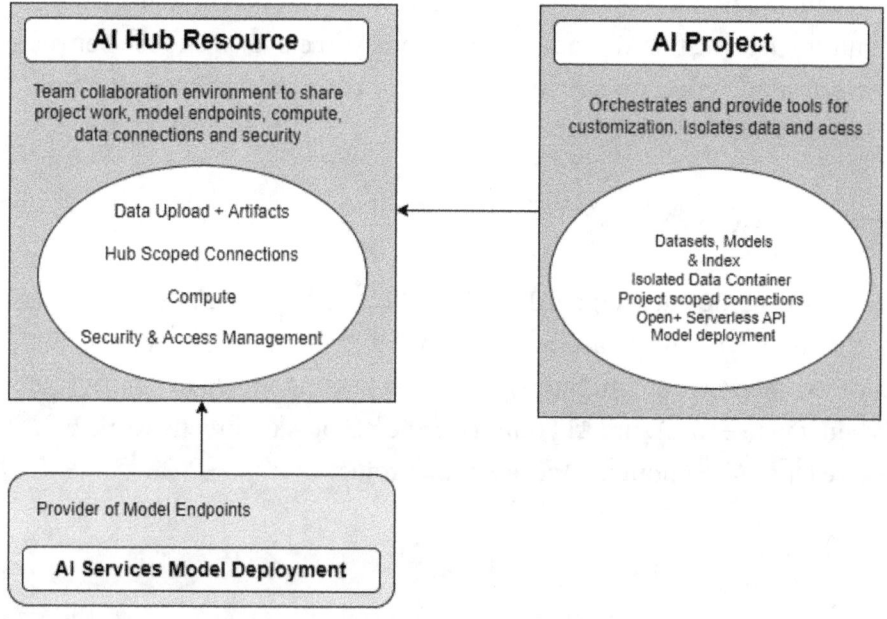

Figure 1-9. *Azure AI Foundry architecture*

As you can see, when you create an Azure AI Foundry instance, it creates an Azure AI hub resource, which is a top-level environment consisting of data upload and storing artifacts, all connections in the bounded context of the hub, compute resources, and security management and governance. So all these components are managed at a top level of the Azure AI Foundry instance. An Azure AI hub can have multiple AI projects. These AI projects completely orchestrate artifacts and components of a specific project/AI model. Projects consist of datasets, models, indexes, and API deployments.

So with this setup, you can have multiple projects in an Azure AI hub. But, they can use the same computer and security configurations, and these projects can have different datasets, models, and indexes. You can also invite users at a project level to collaborate in Azure AI Foundry. During the AI model deployment, you can also choose between serverless and computer. Azure AI Foundry consists of the components discussed next.

Azure OpenAI

It consists of the latest OpenAI models. With Azure OpenAI, you can create secure deployments. It also has playgrounds to do the experiments, fine-tune the models, content filters, and batch jobs, as shown in Figure 1-10. When you use the Azure AI Foundry project, you can directly work with Azure OpenAI without an Azure Studio project.

CHAPTER 1   GETTING STARTED WITH AZURE AI FOUNDRY

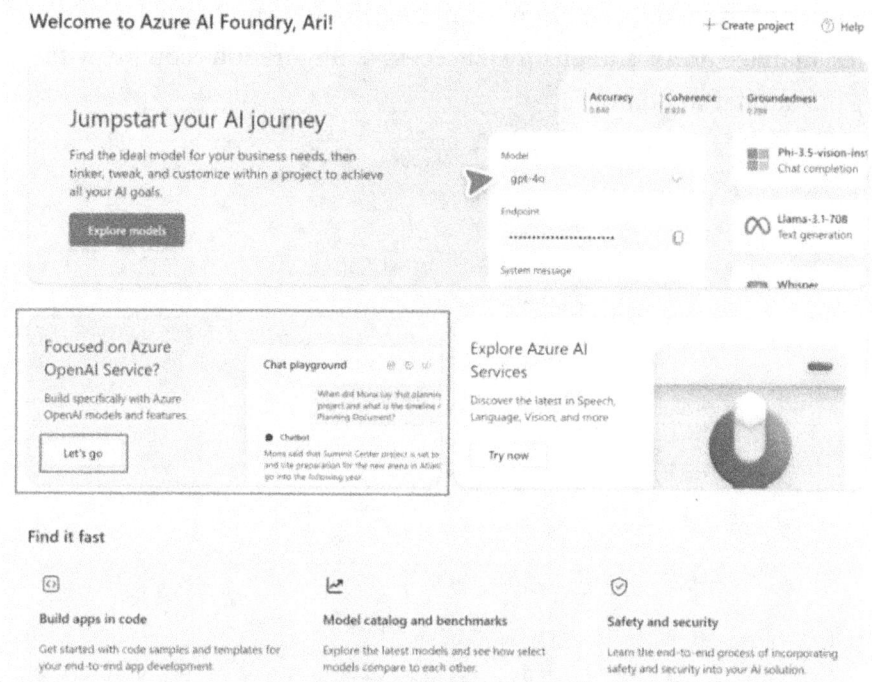

Figure 1-10. *Azure OpenAI model*

Azure OpenAI provides REST API access to OpenAI's powerful language models.

Management Center

It is a part of Azure AI Foundry, which mainly takes care of overall management and governance activities. You can manage Azure AI Foundry hubs, projects, resources, and settings as shown in Figure 1-11. Use **All hubs + projects** to view all hubs and projects you can access. Use the **Project** sections in the left menu to manage individual hubs and projects. You can view and manage quotas and usage metrics across multiple hubs and Azure subscriptions. Using the Quota link, you can

CHAPTER 1   GETTING STARTED WITH AZURE AI FOUNDRY

view and manage quotas. From the management center, you can assign roles, manage users, and ensure all access configurations comply with organizational standards.

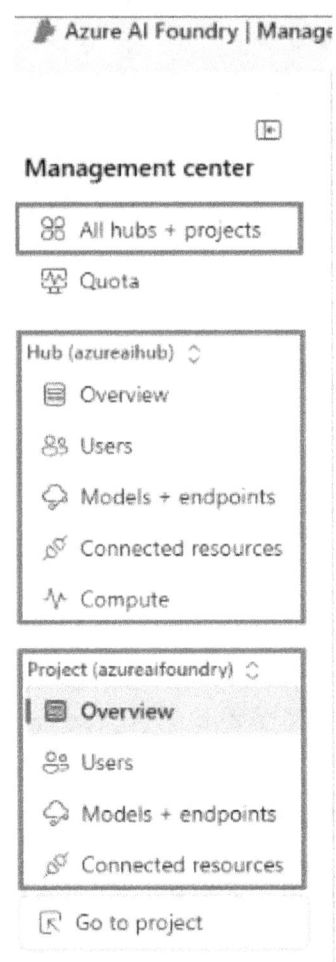

Figure 1-11. *Azure AI Foundry management center*

CHAPTER 1   GETTING STARTED WITH AZURE AI FOUNDRY

Azure AI Foundry Hub

An Azure AI Foundry hub is the highest layer in the AI Foundry portal and provides a platform to centralize security, connectivity, and computing resources. This layer is set up based on Azure machine learning services. When the AI Foundry hub is created, AI developers can create projects and access shared resources without additional access or administration.

Projects created inside the AI Foundry hub inherit the same security configurations and access to shared resources, similar to access at the hub level. Teams can internally organize the project workspace as needed and restrict or isolate access to data.

As you can see from Figure 1-12, you can go to the management center, click **All hubs + projects**, and click **New project ➤ New hub**.

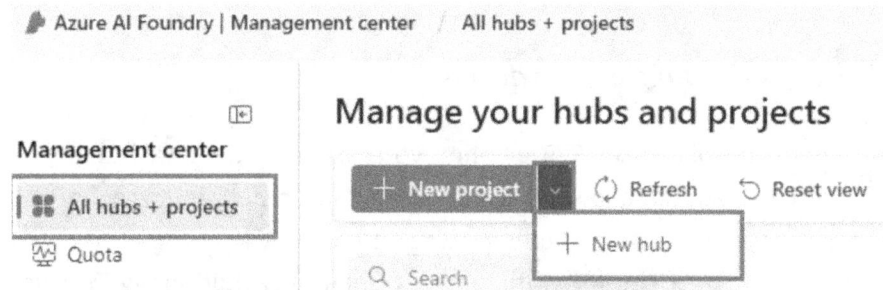

Figure 1-12. *Create new hub*

Once you create a new hub, a dialog box opens where you must enter all details, as shown in Figure 1-13.

17

CHAPTER 1 GETTING STARTED WITH AZURE AI FOUNDRY

```
Create a new hub

① Create a hub                 Create a hub for your projects
                               A hub is the collaboration environment for your t
② Review and finish            connections, and security settings.

                               Do you need to customize security or the depend
                               Hub name *
                               ┌─────────────────────────────────────────────┐
                               │ contoso-hub                                 │
                               └─────────────────────────────────────────────┘
                               Subscription * ⓘ
                               ┌─────────────────────────────────────────────┐
                               │ contoso                                     │
                               └─────────────────────────────────────────────┘
                               Resource group * ⓘ
                               ┌─────────────────────────────────────────────┐
                               │ (new) rg-contoso                            │
                               └─────────────────────────────────────────────┘
```

Figure 1-13. Configure hub details

If your company uses Azure Policy, you can set up a secure hub in the Azure portal that meets the company's requirements. For a secure hub, you need to integrate it either using Azure Key Vault or using the Microsoft-managed identity with network isolation. Additionally, you also need to enable encryption. However, default encryption is enabled with Microsoft-managed keys, and you can also use customer-managed keys. You can manage an Azure AI Foundry hub using the features described in Table 1-2.

Table 1-2. *AI Foundry Hub Capabilities*

Feature	Description
Security configurations	Enables encryption with customer-managed keys and implements restricted network access and user access management
Connections	Provides access to external resources to AI developers without exposing any credentials to individuals
Compute and quota allocations	Shares compute capability across all projects in AI Foundry
AI service access keys	Endpoints to access foundational models like Azure OpenAI, Azure AI Speech, Azure AI Vision, and Azure AI Content Safety
Policy	Sets policy for all the projects within the hub
Dependent Azure resources	Stores artifacts that are generated while working with the AI Foundry hub

Azure AI Foundry Project

An Azure AI Foundry project is a part of an Azure AI Foundry hub. `Microsoft.MachineLearningServices/workspaces` is the Azure resource provider for a project. A project is an organizational container to allow AI developers to organize their work, save state across tools like prompt flows, and collaborate. A hub can contain multiple projects, and one project can have multiple users. This layer of the project inside the AI Foundry hub can track billing, manage access, and enable data isolation. An Azure AI Foundry project is used for

- Building and customizing AI applications
- Setting up reusable components using datasets, models, and indexes

- Securing and bounding the context container to upload and manage data

- Reusable and shared project-scoped connections

- Open-source model deployments from the catalog and fine-tuning

Inside the project, you can organize various components in the Azure AI Foundry portal.

- **Data**: Datasets to create indexes, validate, and fine-tune models

- **Flows**: Implementation of AI logic

- **Evaluations**: Validate and evaluate the model or flow based on the metrics

- **Indexes**: Vector search indexes based on your data

- **Project connections**: Connection to external resources that you can use in Azure AI Foundry and that can be used by all project members

- **Prompt flow runtime**: Generate, customize, and execute the prompt flows

Connections

Connections in an Azure AI Foundry hub can access and consume both Microsoft and non-Microsoft resources within AI Foundry projects. Connections can be created for one project but can be reused across all projects within the AI Foundry hub. As you can see in Figure 1-14, from the Azure AI Foundry portal, using the connected resources, you can click **New connection** to create the connection.

Figure 1-14. *Create connections in Azure AI Foundry*

You can create various service connections in the Azure AI Foundry portal.

- Azure AI Search
- Azure Blob Storage
- Azure Data Lake Storage Gen2
- Azure Content Safety
- Azure OpenAI
- Serverless model

CHAPTER 1   GETTING STARTED WITH AZURE AI FOUNDRY

- Microsoft OneLake
- API Key
- Custom

You can use either API or custom keys to connect to non-Azure services.

Conclusion

This chapter laid the foundation for understanding Azure AI Foundry and its critical role in the evolving landscape of generative AI. You explored the fundamentals of generative AI, emphasizing how AI models generate human-like text, images, and more. Additionally, you delved into the art of prompt engineering, a critical skill for maximizing AI capabilities.

Azure AI Foundry was introduced, covering its key features and how it simplifies AI adoption. Finally, you examined its architecture, providing a structured overview of its components and how they interact to deliver robust AI solutions.

With this foundational knowledge, it's time to take the next step—exploring Azure AI Foundry. The next chapter dives into Azure AI Foundry's environment, seamless integration with Azure OpenAI, model benchmarking, deployments, and more. Let's unlock the full potential of Azure AI Foundry as you embark on this hands-on journey!

CHAPTER 2

Exploring Azure AI Foundry

After reading Chapter 1, you are acquainted with Azure AI Foundry's power and how it provides a unified platform for AI developers to build, develop, and deploy GenAI-based applications. Imagine having the power to build AI solutions with just a few clicks—without needing a PhD in machine learning. That's the promise of Azure AI Foundry.

Roll up your sleeves; it's time to dive into the platform, setting up an AI environment and having a firsthand experience with Azure OpenAI. You'll learn how to explore model catalogs, benchmark performance, and seamlessly deploy models. You'll also get hands-on with the chat playground, experimenting with different prompts and learning how the prompt catalog can supercharge your AI workflows.

By the end of this chapter, you'll have a solid foundation to start building with Azure AI Foundry—let's get started!

This chapter covers the following topics.

- Setting up your AI environment
- Connecting Azure OpenAI to an AI Foundry hub
- Exploring model catalogs, benchmarking, and deployment
- Getting hands-on experience with a chat playground
- Understanding prompt catalogs

CHAPTER 2   EXPLORING AZURE AI FOUNDRY

Setting up Your AI Environment

Many people consider Azure AI Foundry related only to the generative AI space. But it is more than that. It is a whole new horizon to create a completely new AI experience, supporting existing predictive AI experiences and the new state-of-the-art Azure OpenAI resources supporting generative AI applications for your enterprise. Now, let's look at how to set up an Azure AI Foundry environment.

To create an Azure AI Foundry hub, go to **portal.azure.com**, and search for the Azure AI Foundry resource, as shown in Figure 2-1.

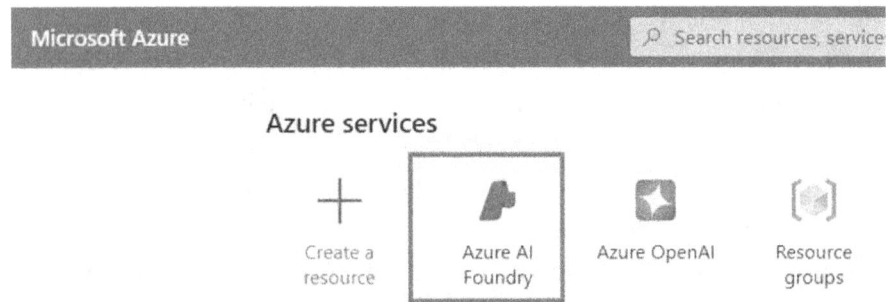

Figure 2-1. *Azure Marketplace: Azure AI Foundry resource*

Once you are on the Azure AI Foundry home page, you can create a project or a hub, as shown in Figure 2-2. Click the **Create** button and select the **Hub** option to create an AI Foundry hub.

CHAPTER 2 EXPLORING AZURE AI FOUNDRY

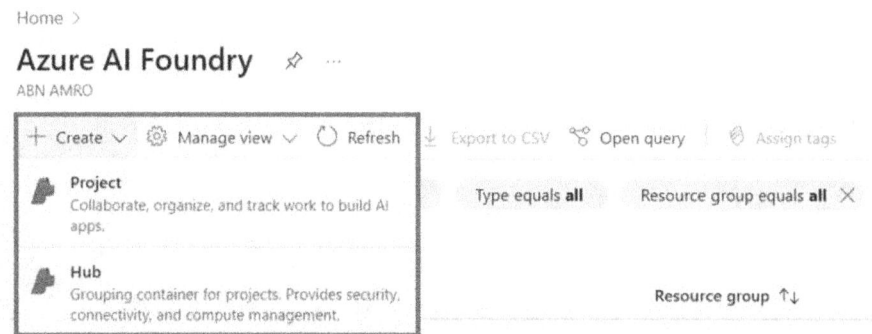

Figure 2-2. *Create an Azure AI Foundry hub*

Once you create the hub, a dialog box opens for you to provide more information, as shown in Figure 2-3.

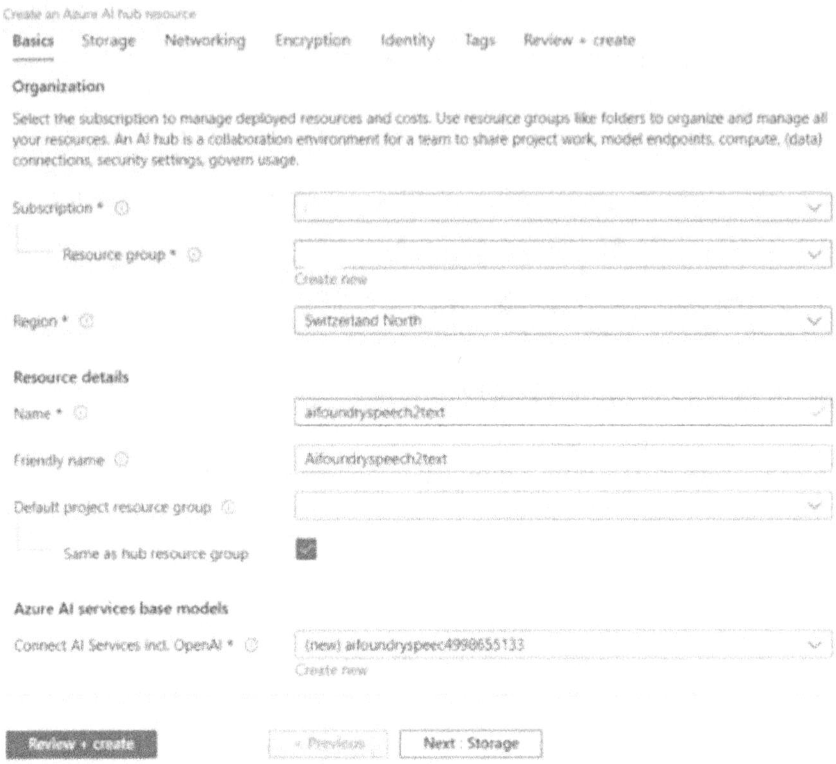

CHAPTER 2   EXPLORING AZURE AI FOUNDRY

Figure 2-3. AI Foundry hub configurations

You must enter the following basic information to configure an AI Foundry hub.

- **Subscription** and **Resource group**: Provide the Azure subscription and resource group for the hub.

- **Region**: Provide the region to deploy the hub to.

- **Name** and **Friendly name**: Provide the resource name.

CHAPTER 2   EXPLORING AZURE AI FOUNDRY

- **Default project resource group**: Select the resource group; you can use the same resource group as the hub resource group.

- **Azure AI services base models**: Choose the Azure AI service to connect.

Click **Next: Storage** to provide storage information, as displayed in Figure 2-4.

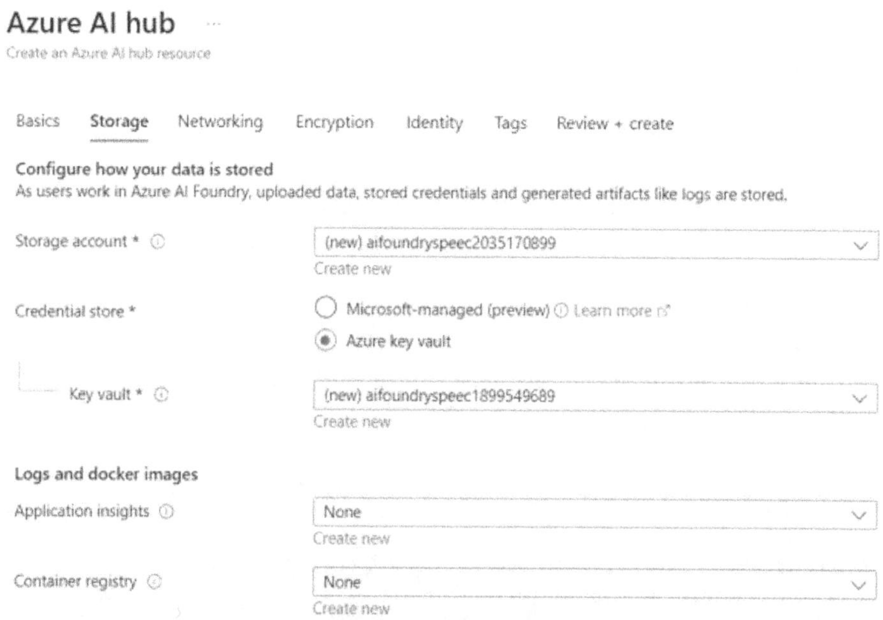

Figure 2-4. Azure AI hub storage configuration

The next step is to set up networking for your AI Foundry hub. As shown in Figure 2-5, there are multiple ways to configure networking. You need to configure Inbound and Outbound access.

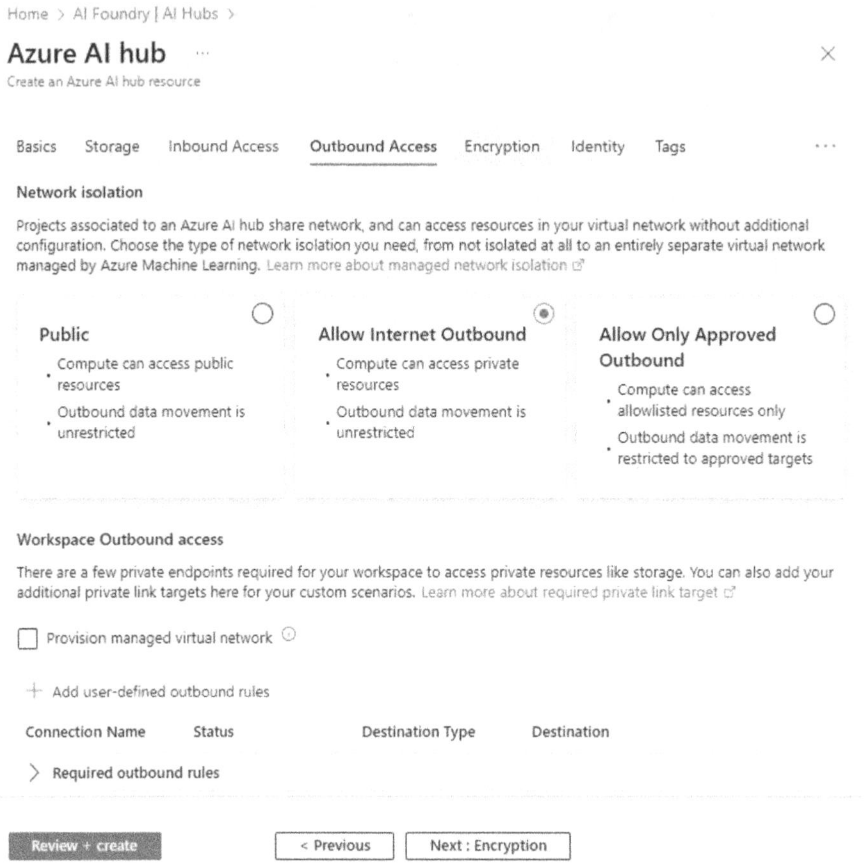

CHAPTER 2 EXPLORING AZURE AI FOUNDRY

Figure 2-5. AI Foundry hub networking configuration

- **Public**: With this configuration, the workspace can be accessed via a public endpoint. There is no restriction on the outbound data movement, and compute resources can be accessed publicly. This is the least secure and preferred option for configuring your AI Foundry hub.

CHAPTER 2   EXPLORING AZURE AI FOUNDRY

- **Allow Internet Outbound**: Workspace can only be accessed via a private endpoint and the compute resources. However, outbound data movement is not restricted and is public.

- **Allow Only Approved Outbound**: This configuration is most secure and preferable where access to private endpoints, compute resources, and data is only accessible to the whitelisted or approved targets.

After network configuration setup, the next step is to configure encryption as shown in Figure 2-6. Note that you can't change the encryption key setting once the workspace is created.

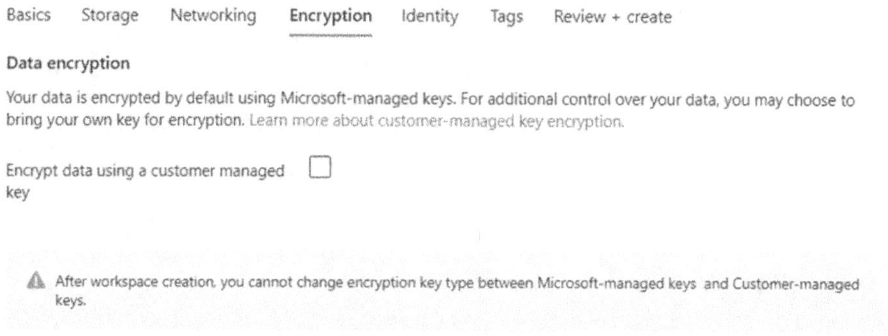

| Basics | Storage | Networking | **Encryption** | Identity | Tags | Review + create |

Data encryption

Your data is encrypted by default using Microsoft-managed keys. For additional control over your data, you may choose to bring your own key for encryption. Learn more about customer-managed key encryption.

Encrypt data using a customer managed key ☐

⚠ After workspace creation, you cannot change encryption key type between Microsoft-managed keys and Customer-managed keys.

Figure 2-6. *Azure AI hub encryption setting*

After setting up encryption, you must configure identities to manage the AI Foundry hub as shown in Figure 2-7. You can either use system-assigned identities or user-assigned identities. Storage account access can be credential-based or identity-based.

29

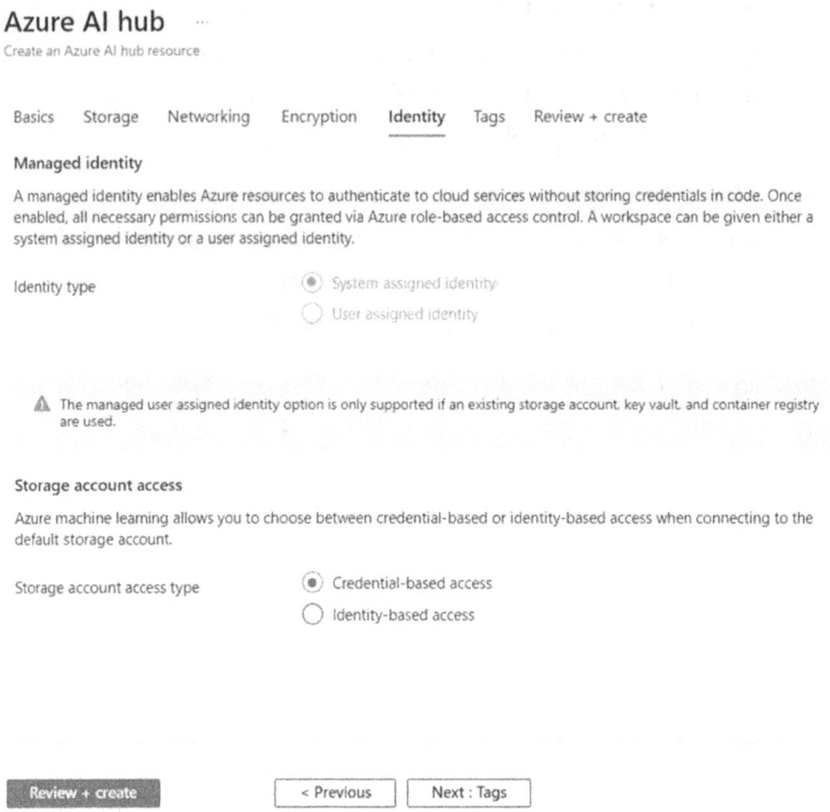

CHAPTER 2   EXPLORING AZURE AI FOUNDRY

Figure 2-7. Identity configuration for AI Foundry hub

After entering all details, the final step is to click the **Review + create** button. It then shows you a complete overview of all the filled information, and once you submit, the AI Foundry hub is created within a couple of minutes (see Figure 2-8).

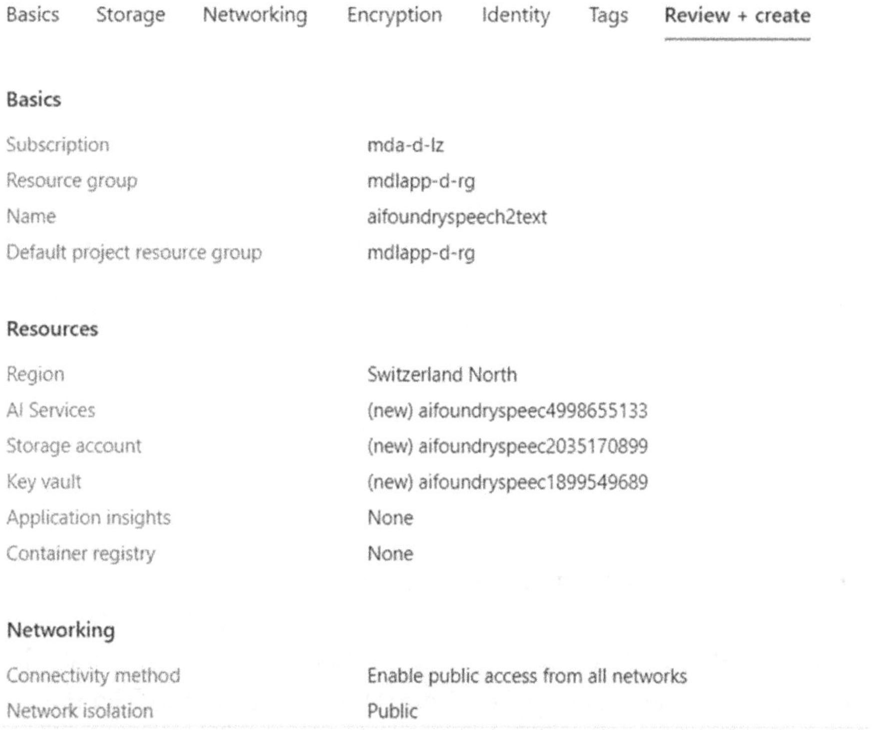

CHAPTER 2   EXPLORING AZURE AI FOUNDRY

Basics	Storage	Networking	Encryption	Identity	Tags	**Review + create**

Basics

Subscription	mda-d-lz
Resource group	mdlapp-d-rg
Name	aifoundryspeech2text
Default project resource group	mdlapp-d-rg

Resources

Region	Switzerland North
AI Services	(new) aifoundryspeec4998655133
Storage account	(new) aifoundryspeec2035170899
Key vault	(new) aifoundryspeec1899549689
Application insights	None
Container registry	None

Networking

Connectivity method	Enable public access from all networks
Network isolation	Public

Figure 2-8. *Review + create AI Foundry hub*

Now, you can create a project inside the Azure AI Foundry hub. After a project is created, when you click **Overview**, as shown in Figure 2-9, you can see the API endpoint and keys, which can be used for various purposes.

CHAPTER 2   EXPLORING AZURE AI FOUNDRY

Figure 2-9. *AI Foundry project creation*

You can also use this Azure OpenAI endpoint to build generative AI applications. But let's set up a new Azure OpenAI instance and connect it to an AI Foundry hub.

Connecting Azure OpenAI to AI Foundry Hub

This section deploys an Azure OpenAI resource in the Azure portal, builds GPT models in Azure OpenAI to build generative applications, and connects them to the Azure AI Foundry hub. There are multiple ways to use Azure OpenAI within the Azure resource group.

CHAPTER 2   EXPLORING AZURE AI FOUNDRY

Use Azure OpenAI Outside an Azure AI Foundry Project

If you have an existing Azure OpenAI model in the Azure AI Foundry portal, it is simple to use the OpenAI model outside a project.

Go to the Azure AI Foundry home page. In the **Focused on Azure OpenAI Service?** section and click **Let's go**. Figure 2-10 is an overview of the Azure portal.

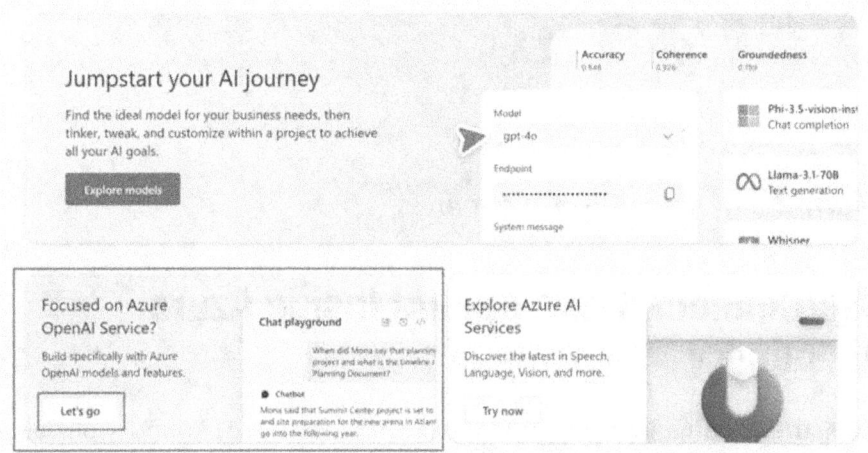

Figure 2-10. *Azure OpenAI service page*

Figure 2-11 shows an overview of existing Azure OpenAI resources.

CHAPTER 2   EXPLORING AZURE AI FOUNDRY

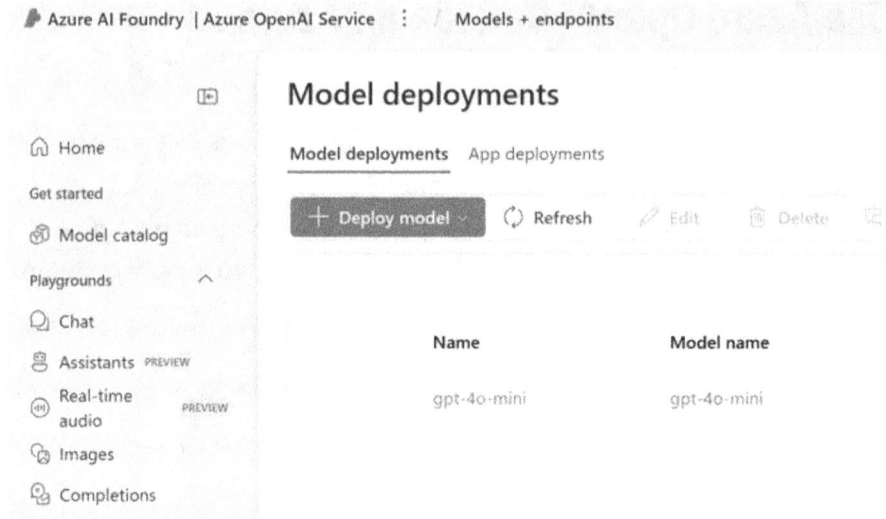

Figure 2-11. Azure OpenAI resources

Use/Connect Azure OpenAI Inside Azure AI Foundry

Using the existing Azure OpenAI service in the Azure AI Foundry portal is also possible.

While creating the project for the first time in the Azure AI Foundry hub, you can select or create existing Azure services, including Azure OpenAI.

If the AI Foundry project has already been created, you can connect your existing Azure OpenAI resource. First, go to the Azure AI Foundry project and select **Management center**. In the project, select **Connected resources**, and then click **New connection**, as shown in Figure 2-12.

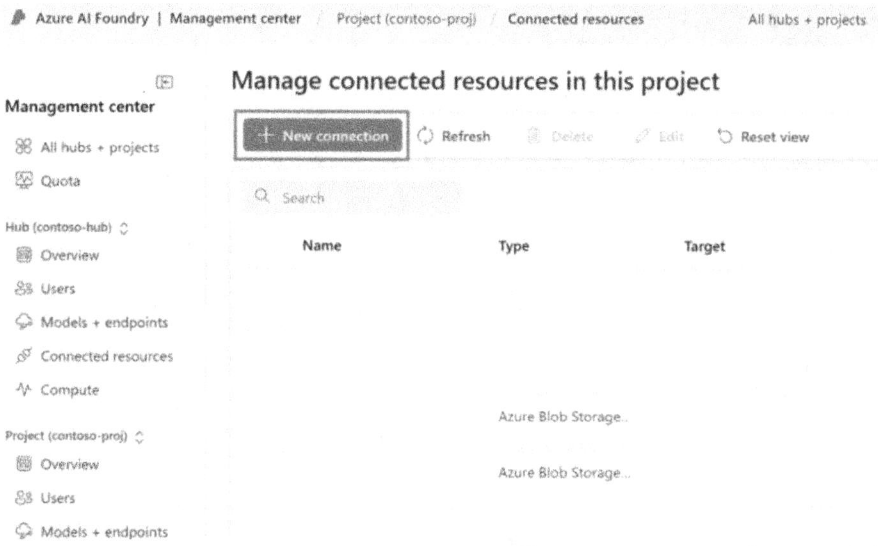

CHAPTER 2   EXPLORING AZURE AI FOUNDRY

Figure 2-12. *AI Foundry project: add connection to external asset*

Select the Azure AI service that you want to connect to a project (see Figure 2-13).

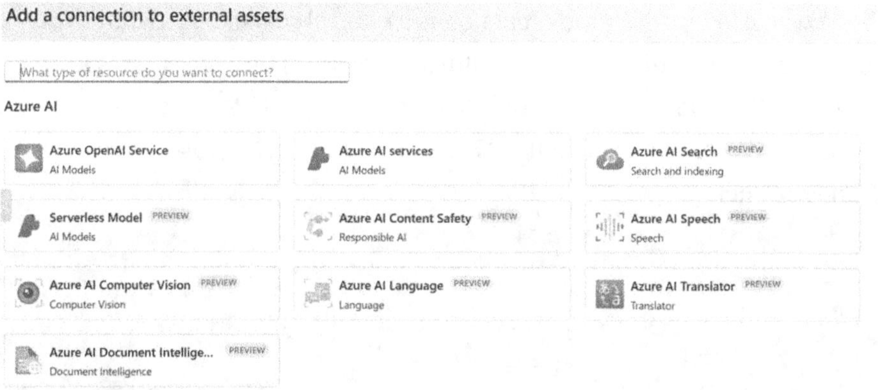

Figure 2-13. *Add connection to external assets*

After selecting the Azure service you want to connect to, click the **Add connection** button, as shown in Figure 2-14.

CHAPTER 2   EXPLORING AZURE AI FOUNDRY

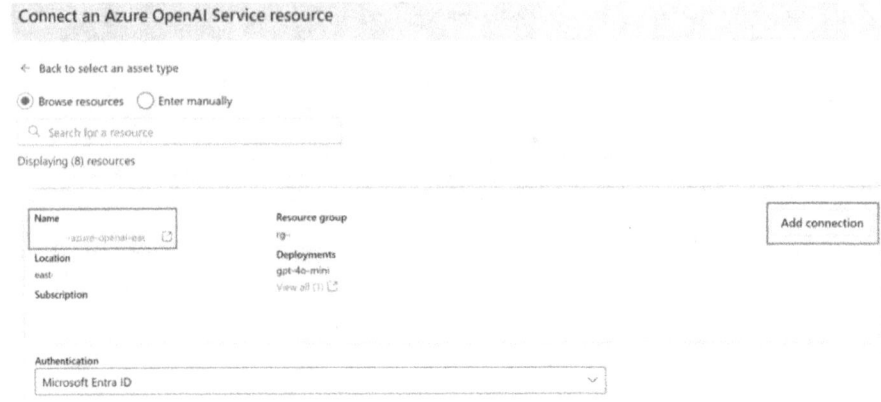

Figure 2-14. Connect to Azure OpenAI service

Exploring Model Catalogs, Benchmarking, and Deployment

Model Catalogs

The Azure AI Foundry model catalog is a central place to find and use a wide variety of models to build generative AI applications (see Figure 2-15). It has a lot of models from various providers like Azure OpenAI, Mistral, Meta, NVIDIA, Hugging Face, and Microsoft-trained models.

CHAPTER 2   EXPLORING AZURE AI FOUNDRY

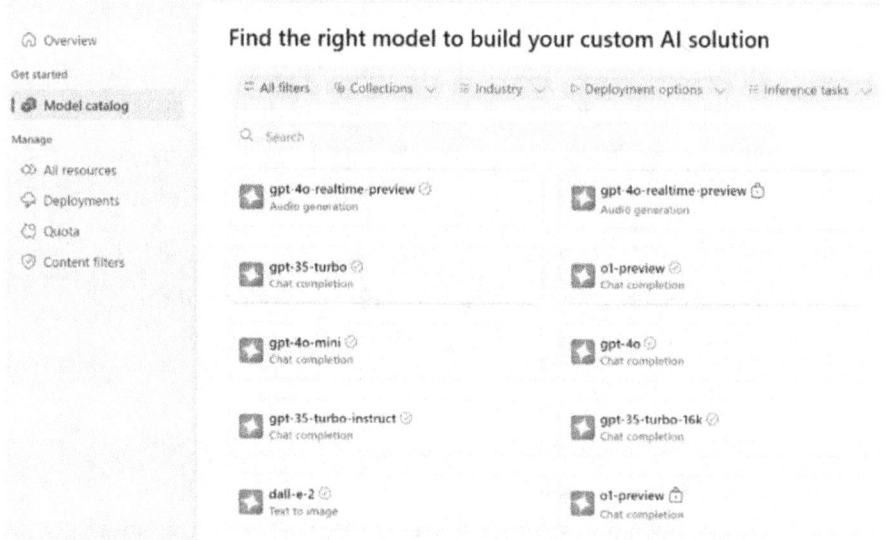

Figure 2-15. *AI Foundry model catalog*

All models in the AI Foundry model catalog support global standard deployment types. It supports the following model families.

- AI21 Labs
- Azure OpenAI
- Cohere
- Core42
- DeepSeek
- Meta
- Microsoft
- Mistral
- NTT Data

The model catalog organizes models into different collections.

- **Models from partners**: All the widely available partner models are available on the Azure AI platform. When you deploy the models in the Azure AI Foundry portal, their availability is subject to Microsoft's service level agreement.

- **Azure OpenAI models exclusively on Azure**: All the leading models are available when integrating with Azure OpenAI.

- **Open models from the Hugging Face**: Hundreds of models from Hugging Face hubs are also available in the model catalog of Azure AI Foundry.

Using the model catalog, you can search and discover models using the filters and keyword search. It also offers model performance benchmark metrics for selected models. On the model catalog model cards, you can find the following.

- **Quick facts**: Quick insights on the key information about the model

- **Details**: Detailed information about the model, including version, description, and supported data type

- **Benchmarks**: Performance benchmark metrics for models (see Figure 2-16)

CHAPTER 2   EXPLORING AZURE AI FOUNDRY

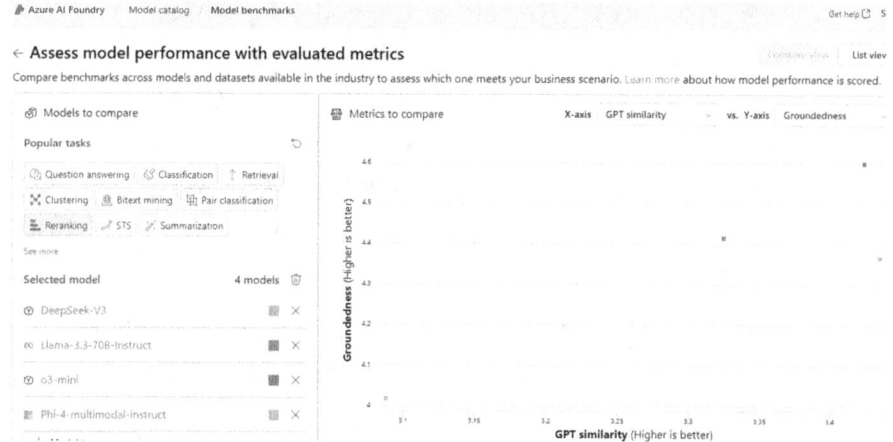

Figure 2-16. *Model benchmarking in Azure AI Foundry*

- **Code samples**: Basic sample code to get started with AI application development
- **License**: Legal information about the model licensing
- **Artifacts**: View and download the model assets using the user interface only for open models

There are two ways to deploy models in the model catalog: managed compute and serverless API.

- **Managed compute**: In the managed compute deployment experience, models are deployed to the dedicated virtual machines. Cost for the compute resources is calculated based on the virtual machine core hours, which are used by deployment hours. Managed compute supports key-based authentication and Microsoft Entra authentication, providing a secure, enterprise-level authentication option. It also uses Azure AI content safety service APIs without any extra cost.

39

- **Serverless API**: In serverless API model deployment, access to the model is given through the deployment, which provisions an API to access the model. Cost is calculated based on the inputs and outputs to the API, in the form of tokens. It only supports keys for API authentication. It is compatible with Azure Content Safety, but billing is done separately.

Models in the model catalog are continuously refreshed with the latest updated and newer capable models. Depending on the update from the model provider about the model, you might need to update/replace models available in the catalog for your generative AI application. Models in the model catalog can have one of the following stages.

- **Preview**: Models with label preview are experimental in nature. It is not guaranteed that models that are in preview can become generally available. So, these models should only be used for experimentation purposes.

- **Generally available**: The default status for models in the model catalog is generally available. In the model catalog, if the lifecycle status is not labeled, then its status is generally available. Generally, the available model weights and APIs are fixed.

- **Legacy**: Legacy models are meant to be deprecated. A new, better model available in the same model family is one example of a model you should plan to switch to. Existing model deployments remain functional throughout the legacy stage, and new model deployments can be made up to the deprecation date.

CHAPTER 2   EXPLORING AZURE AI FOUNDRY

- **Deprecated**: Models with the label deprecated are not available for the model deployments. Until they are retired, you can continue working and deploying with these types of models if they already exist, but you can't use them for new deployments.

- **Retired**: Models labeled as retired are no longer available for use. You can neither use it for existing models nor for new models.

Model Benchmarking

In the Azure AI Foundry portal, you can compare different types of benchmarks for AI models. While working or building generative applications, if you are experimenting or have already decided which model to use, it is best to compare various model benchmarks, validate them against your business scenario, and make informed decisions.

As highlighted in Figure 2-17, Collections lets you filter or choose which models you want to select. If you want to compare benchmarks across different models, click the **Compare models** button.

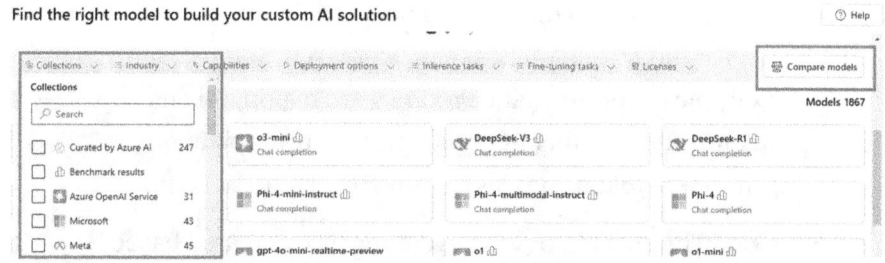

Figure 2-17. AI Foundry model benchmarking

In Azure AI Foundry, model benchmarks evaluate large language models (LLMs) and small language models (SLMs) in the following four categories.

41

- **Quality**: Azure AI evaluates the models based on accuracy and prompt-based metrics. Accuracy scores are available both at the dataset level and at model levels. There are various subcategories for prompt-based metrics, as described in Table 2-1.

Table 2-1. Prompt-based Quality Metrics

Metric	Description
Coherence	How well the model generates output, which is human-like language and naturally readable
Fluency	Compliance with the language's grammatical rules, syntax, and the right use of vocabulary
GPTSimilarity	Similarity between the actual practical reality of the sentence and the prediction sentence generated by the AI model
Groundedness	Evaluates the model output with information from the input
Relevance	Relevance of model output to the question in the prompt

- **Performance**: These metrics are calculated as an aggregate over 14 days, based on 24 trials sent daily with an hour interval between every trial. Some examples of performance metrics are region, tokens per minute, number of requests/runs, prompt length, number of tokens processed, tokenizer, and so forth.

- **Cost**: The cost of an Azure AI model is calculated based on the following metrics: cost per input tokens, cost per output tokens, and estimated cost for the sum of cost per input to output tokens with a ratio of 3:1.

CHAPTER 2   EXPLORING AZURE AI FOUNDRY

To view the model benchmarks, go to the AI Foundry home page at https://ai.azure.com/ and select the model. Click **Benchmarks**, as highlighted in Figure 2-18.

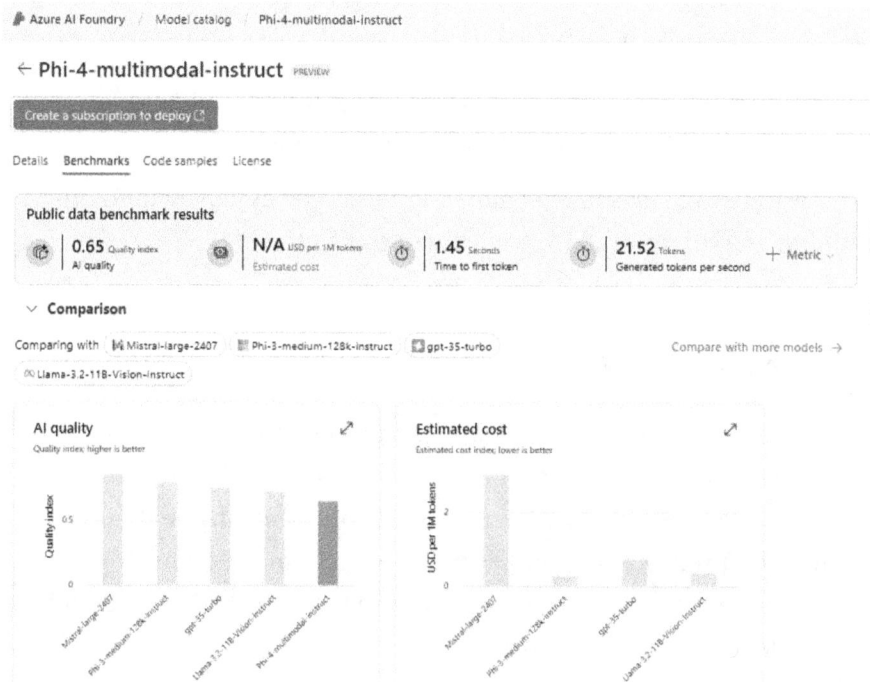

Figure 2-18. *Model benchmarks for Phi-4-multimodal-instruct*

Deployment

There are various types of model deployments based on the model type.

- **Model as a service**: You can deploy a model as a service (MaaS) of your generative AI application. It doesn't need compute power from your Azure subscription or resource group.

- Open and custom models: Using managed infrastructure, you can host open models in your own subscription. The model catalog has many models available from Azure OpenAI, Hugging Face, NVIDIA, and so forth.

- Azure OpenAI models: Enterprise features from Azure, including the latest available OpenAI models

There are two ways in which the model can be deployed in Azure AI Foundry: as a serverless API or managed compute.

Chat Playground

Chat playground is a sandbox or lab environment to learn how your chatbot or GenAI application works in different scenarios before you actually deploy your application to production. Using the chatbot, you can test different prompts and models to see which works best for your use case. Before you access the chat playground in Azure AI Foundry, you must have the following permissions.

- Contributor or owner role in Azure AI Foundry, which is distinct from general Azure roles

- In an existing AI Foundry hub, you should have an AI developer role

The first step is to deploy the model to the project by logging into the AI Foundry portal at https://ai.azure.com/ and selecting the **project** you want. Next, click **Model catalog** and select the model that you want. Click the **Create a subscription to deploy** button, as Figure 2-19 highlights.

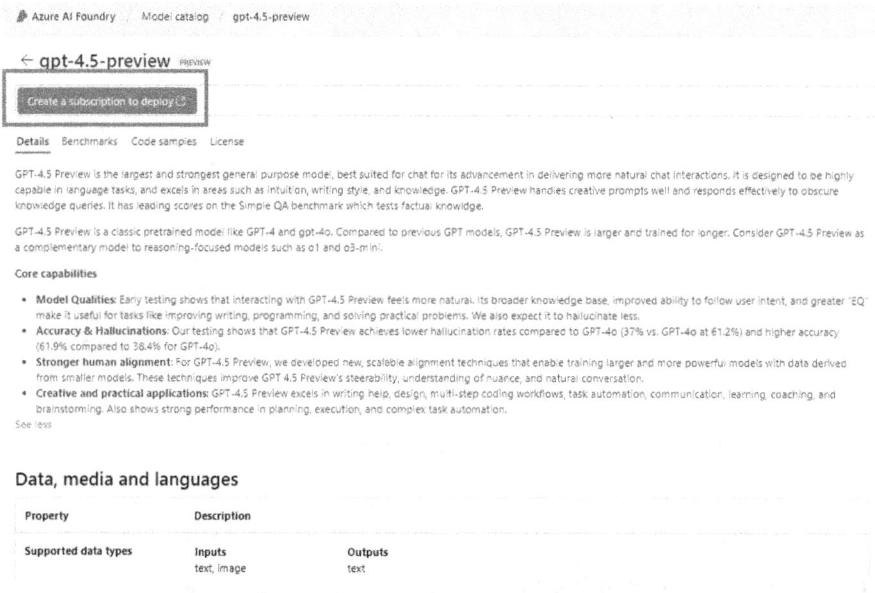

CHAPTER 2 EXPLORING AZURE AI FOUNDRY

Figure 2-19. Deploy model in AI Foundry

Once the model is deployed, open the playground to test the model. Using the chat playground, you can validate and check how the model works with or without data.

You can write a prompt that takes input and produces output in the console. Optionally, add a safety message from prebuilt or customized messages (see Figure 2-20). It provides explicit information to avoid potential responsible AI threats and guides users to interact safely via prompts.

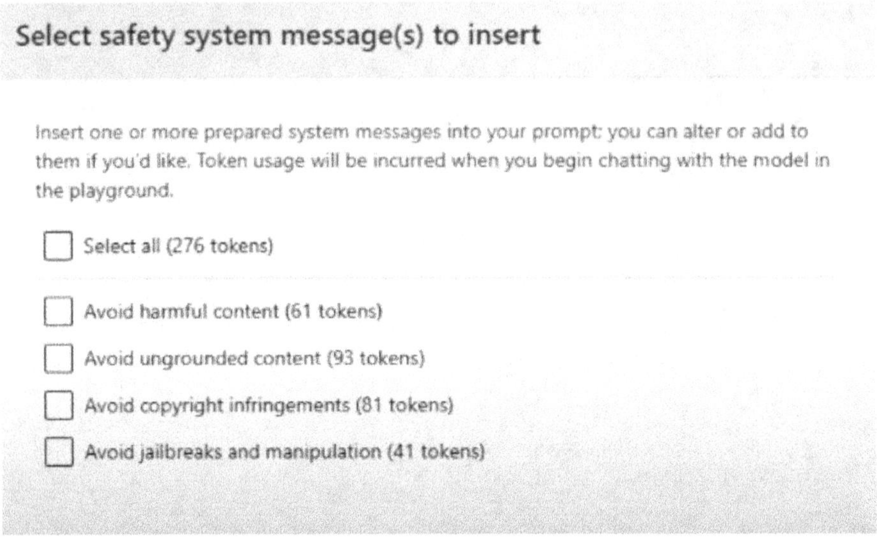

CHAPTER 2   EXPLORING AZURE AI FOUNDRY

Select safety system message(s) to insert

Insert one or more prepared system messages into your prompt; you can alter or add to them if you'd like. Token usage will be incurred when you begin chatting with the model in the playground.

☐ Select all (276 tokens)

☐ Avoid harmful content (61 tokens)

☐ Avoid ungrounded content (93 tokens)

☐ Avoid copyright infringements (81 tokens)

☐ Avoid jailbreaks and manipulation (41 tokens)

Figure 2-20. *Safety messages*

It is also possible to set various parameters while in the chat playground as shown in Figure 2-21.

- Included
- Max response
- Temperature
- Top P

CHAPTER 2   EXPLORING AZURE AI FOUNDRY

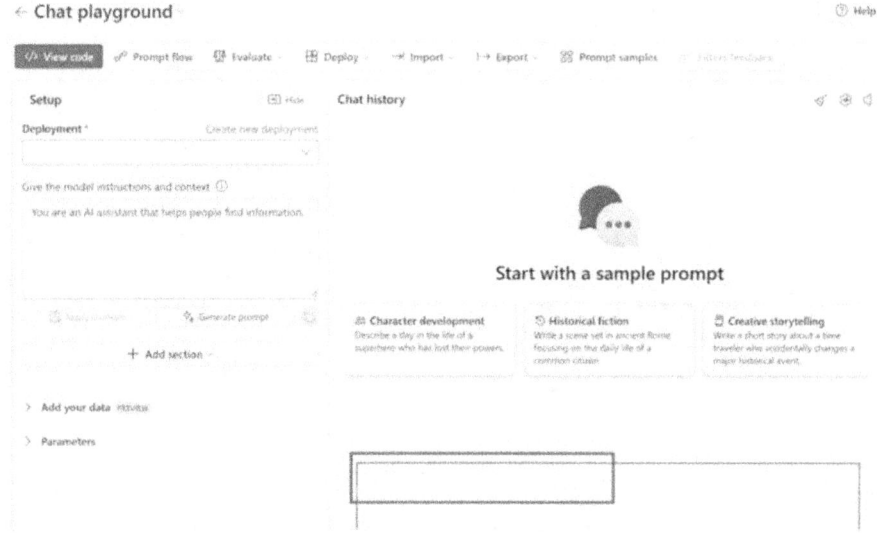

Figure 2-21.   AI Foundry chat playground

In addition to the normal playground to test LLM models, you can access different playgrounds for various purposes, such as speech, images, and industry-specific models, as seen in Figure 2-22.

CHAPTER 2 EXPLORING AZURE AI FOUNDRY

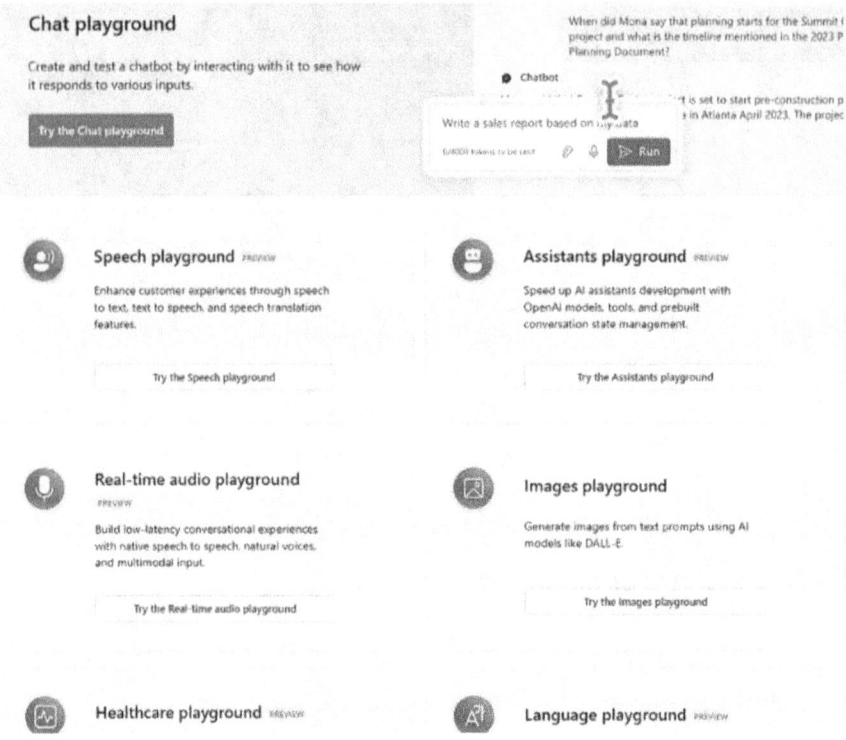

Figure 2-22. *Variety of chat playgrounds*

It is also possible to manually evaluate your model within the playground with the manual inputs. Using the manual evaluation option from the user interface, you can add your input and expected output and evaluate the model response (see Figure 2-23).

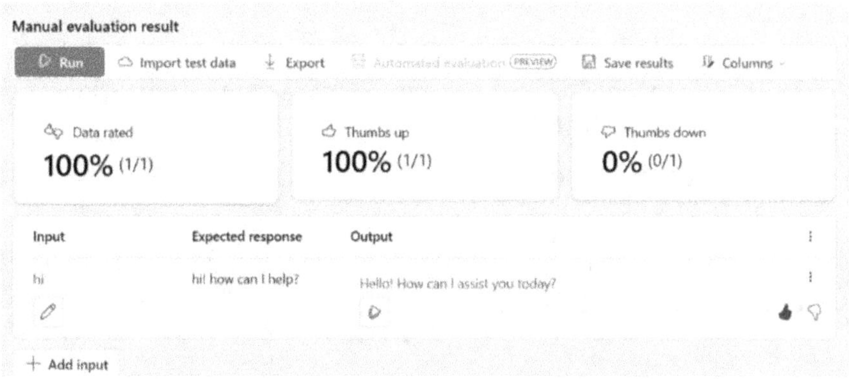

Figure 2-23. Manual evaluation for chat playground

Another major benefit of using chat playground is that once you are done with the experimentation, based on your configurations, it creates code you can use to build your application. It is also possible to export chat settings, which you can use later by importing them to your chat playground. It is also possible to build a chat playground with the AI Foundry SDK.

```
from azure.ai.projects import AIProjectClient
from azure.identity import DefaultAzureCredential

project_connection_string = "<your-connection-string-goes-here>"

project = AIProjectClient.from_connection_string(
    conn_str=project_connection_string, credential=DefaultAzureCredential()
)

chat = project.inference.get_chat_completions_client()
response = chat.complete(
    model="gpt-4o-mini",
    messages=[
```

```
        {
            "role": "system",
            "content": "You are an AI assistant that speaks
            like a techno punk rocker from 2350. Be cool but
            not too cool. Ya dig?",
        },
        {"role": "user", "content": "Hey, can you help me with
my taxes? I'm a freelancer."},
    ],
)

print(response.choices[0].message.content)
```

You can find the connection string from the AI Foundry project overview page. Here, the script uses the hardcoded input and output messages. But in the actual application, the model gets the input from the prompt and produces an output.

In Azure AI Foundry, it is also possible to add data, and based on the data, you can make the model generate output for your input prompt. To add data to your model, click **Add your data ➤ Data source ➤ Upload files**, as shown in Figure 2-24.

CHAPTER 2   EXPLORING AZURE AI FOUNDRY

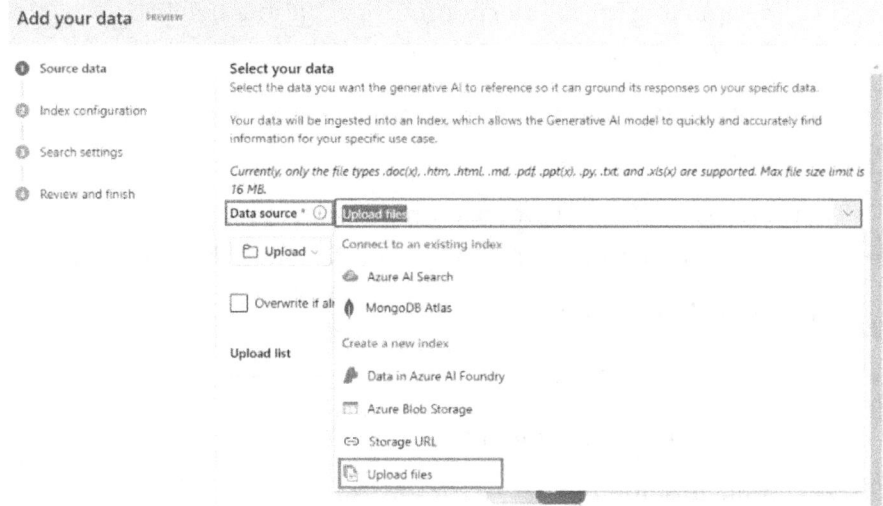

Figure 2-24. *Add your data chat playground*

After uploading the file, select the Azure AI Search service and provide a vector index name to add to it. Once done, you can ask a question in the chat playground. It generates the answer based on the data you uploaded.

Understanding Prompt Catalogs

Before diving into the prompt catalogs, let's examine the basics of prompt engineering. A prompt may be a question or instructions that you can pass to the model with additional information like context or examples. At a very high level, a prompt consists of the following.

- **Instruction**: Specific action that you want your model to execute or perform
- **Context**: Additional context or background (e.g., generate a report)

- **Supporting input information**: Specific and detailed input or questions that you are interested in
- **Output expectation**: Acceptance criteria for the output you need

There are also different types of prompting techniques to effectively design and improve prompts to get a better result from the AI model.

- Zero-shot prompting
- One-shot prompting
- Chain-of-thought prompting
- Meta prompting
- Prompt chaining
- Tree of thoughts
- Retrieval-augmented generation
- Graph prompting
- Active prompting
- Generate knowledge prompting

In Azure AI Foundry, the prompt catalog is a critical feature that helps AI developers and teams standardize, resume, and manage prompts effectively. It is a central repository where GenAI developers can store, organize, and maintain versioning for the prompts, as shown in Figure 2-25. This ensures consistency and a unified view for prompts across the teams.

CHAPTER 2   EXPLORING AZURE AI FOUNDRY

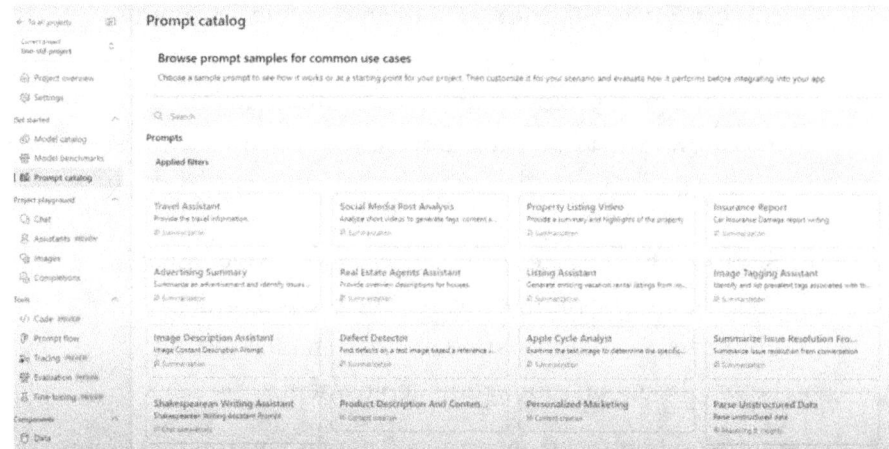

Figure 2-25. *Prompt catalog in Azure AI Foundry*

Let's explore the key features of prompt catalogs in Azure AI Foundry.

- **Centralized prompt management**: Ability to create, store, and share prompts in a well-structured way

- **Version control**: Track and maintain multiple versions of the prompt. You can roll back to any point in time as and when required.

  Tagging: Manage and store prompts based on the metadata, such as use case, model type, and business/domain specification.

- **Predefined templates**: It has a set of predefined templates that are common for common GenAI tasks such as classification, creating a summary, or a listing assistant, and so forth, which can be used.

- **Ease of collaboration**: For prompts stored in the prompt catalog, you can provide role-based access and manage permissions for different prompts. This access management enables ease of collaboration within the team.

53

- **Integration with prompt flows**: Integrating a prompt from the prompt catalog into the prompt flow is also possible. With prompt flow, you can automate AI workflows and reduce manual efforts. Prompt flows are explored in Chapter 3.

  Supports testing: Before the production deployment, you can test the prompts within the catalog, which optimizes the performance and also enables testing before the actual production deployment.

To promote usability and maximize efficiency, you should employ the following practices while creating prompts in the AI Foundry prompt catalog.

- **Use a standard and clear naming convention.** Standard and well-defined naming conventions make the prompt easier to read and fine-tune. While defining a prompt, consider the following.

  – The prompt should be short and descriptive.

  – Use versioning for proper tracking and maintenance.

  For example, use a format like the following.

  {Use Case Name}_{Task}_{Model}_{Version}

  Customerbot_summary_GPT4_V1.1

- **Add tagging.** Proper tags and metadata must be added to enable efficient prompt discovery and retrieval. The following are the recommended tagging information to be defined for the prompts.

  – Use case information

  – Task type

CHAPTER 2 EXPLORING AZURE AI FOUNDRY

- Model information
- Prompt type
- Performance metrics

- **Define a clear and concise prompt.** You can improve the accuracy of the AI model if you create a well-defined and structured prompt. You are recommended to use the following format; you can customize based on your needs.

```
### Context:
Provide a brief introduction to the scenario or data.
Example: "You are an AI assistant for a bank."

### Instruction:
Clearly specify what the model should do.
Example: "Summarize the given financial report in under 100 words."

### Input Format:
Define how the input should be structured.
Example:
- "Report Title: [Title]"
- "Report Body: [Text]"

### Output Format:
Specify the expected response format.
Example:
- "Summary: [Brief summary]"
- "Key Insights: [Bullet points]"

### Constraints:
Set limitations to improve relevance.
Example: "Do not exceed 150 words. Avoid financial jargon."
```

- **Use version tracking.** With version tracking, you can refine prompts over time and roll back to specific versions when required.

  A version strategy might be as follows.

  v 1.0: the initial prompt

  v 1.1: minor change

  v 1.2: major changes

- **Perform prompt testing for performance.** You should measure the following key metrics while testing the prompt before the deployment.
  - Accuracy
  - Consistency
  - Readability
  - Bias and ethics

  You can use the chat playground and test using various testing methods like A/B testing or user feedback loops.

- **Employ automated reviews for governance and compliance.** Ensure data security, privacy, and compliance while managing the prompts in the AI Foundry. You can enable role-based access controls to efficiently and securely manage prompts within and outside the team. You can also enable audit trails to track prompt modifications and changes.

Conclusion

This chapter explored the foundational steps required to set up and operate within the Azure AI Foundry ecosystem. It began by configuring our AI environment, ensuring a seamless connection between Azure OpenAI and an AI Foundry hub. It delved into the model catalog, examining various models, their benchmarking capabilities, and deployment strategies. Additionally, you explored the chat playground, providing a hands-on approach to interacting with AI, and gained insights into prompt cataloging, which is crucial in refining AI-driven responses.

The next chapter explores how Microsoft prompt flows streamline the creation and management of AI workflows, and dives into practical applications such as web classification, API integrations, and advanced function calling techniques.

CHAPTER 3

Building with Prompt Flow

The previous chapter explored the foundations of Azure AI Foundry, setting up the environment, connecting Azure OpenAI, and navigating key components like model catalogs, benchmarking, and deployment. You also got hands-on experience with the chat playground and prompt catalogs, laying the groundwork for effectively using AI models within the Foundry ecosystem.

Let's take the next step by building with a Microsoft prompt flow—a powerful tool designed to create structured AI workflows.

By the end of this chapter, you'll have a solid foundation for building simple and advanced Microsoft prompt flows.

This chapter covers the following topics.

- An introduction to Microsoft prompt flows
- Creating simple I/O flows in AI Foundry
- Understanding the Copilot stack
- Web classification using a prompt flow
- Integrating external APIs with AI Foundry
- Function calling and advanced workflows

CHAPTER 3　BUILDING WITH PROMPT FLOW

Introduction to Prompt Flows

A prompt flow is a tool that helps you design, test, and optimize how AI models respond to user inputs/prompts. Using the prompt flow, you can streamline the complete development lifecycle of AI applications using large language models (LLMs). It is an end-to-end solution that simplifies the process of prototyping, experimenting, and deploying your generative AI application. So it is more about integrating your large language model operations (LLMOps) with Azure DevOps. So when you develop your AI application, there are small components like the endpoint of your application to classify your web URLs, which uses the power of LLMs, you can use prompt flow. With a prompt flow, you can integrate your machine learning operations (MLOps) with DevOps tools, like Azure DevOps or GitHub. It allows for collaboration, so you can build your prototypes for your experiments. It visually represents the flow's setup, allowing users to easily understand the flow and implementation. It is also possible to compare various prompt flows, so you can create and choose to optimize them.

Prompt Flow = Prompt (Collection of input send to model with supporting info) + Flow(Executable instruction to trigger AI Logic)

Let's also look at the lifecycle of prompt flow in more detail. As you can see in Figure 3-1, a prompt flow follows a lifecycle for the seamless development of building generative AI applications. You can create production-ready AI applications by going through the life cycle process of developing, testing, deploying, and tuning the AI model.

CHAPTER 3   BUILDING WITH PROMPT FLOW

Prompt Flow Lifecycle

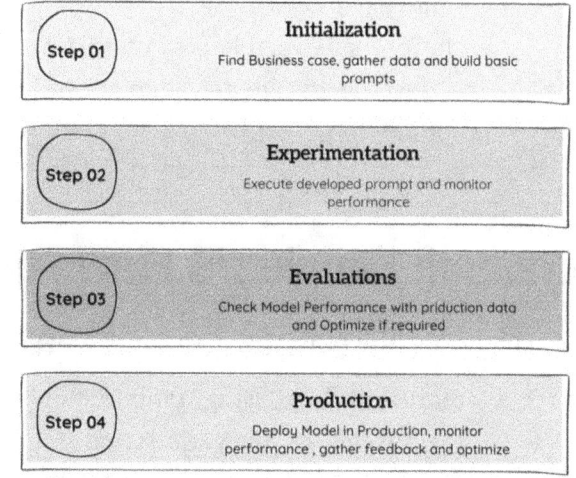

Figure 3-1. *Prompt flow lifecycle*

With prompt flows, you can debug, share, and iterate flows and compare performance while collaborating with the team. A prompt flow is available independently as an open source project on GitHub with its own software development kit (SDK) and Visual Studio Code extension.

Let's also discuss the prompt flow features in Azure AI Foundry.

- **Simplified collaboration**: Multiple users can work on the prompt engineering projects, share knowledge, collaborate, and maintain version control.

- **Unified platform**: It provides a platform for AI developers to manage the full AI development lifecycle, from prompt creation and fine-tuning to evaluation, deployment, and performance monitoring. Flows can be deployed as Azure AI endpoints or integrated into applications via REST APIs. Performance metrics such as latency and accuracy can be monitored for continuous optimization.

- **Enterprise readiness**: It provides secure, comprehensive, reliable enterprise-ready solutions to develop, design, test, deploy, and monitor AI applications.

Creating Simple I/O Flows in AI Foundry

You can create different types of prompt flows in AI Foundry.

- **Standard flow**: Using standard flow, you can create various flows using various tools for developing LLM applications. It is mainly used for general application development.

- **Chat flow**: Chat flows are mainly used for conversational application development. It is built on the standard flow and provides out-of-the-box support for chat input and output. Using chat flow, you can seamlessly develop applications with a conversational context.

- **Evaluation flow**: Using the evaluation flow, you can evaluate the performance of previous prompt flows and provide outcomes with various metrics to measure the overall assessment and improvement of the model.

The following are the prerequisites for a prompt flow.

- Azure subscription
- Hub-based project in AI Foundry
- Create a compute session
- Configure access to storage account (assign a storage blob data contributor role)

CHAPTER 3   BUILDING WITH PROMPT FLOW

Once prerequisites are set up, to create a prompt flow, you can go to the AI Foundry portal, select the project, and select prompt flow, as shown in Figure 3-2.

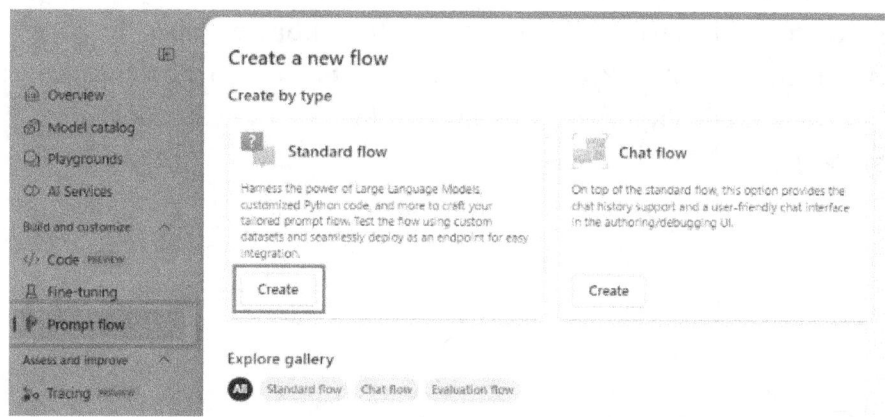

Figure 3-2. *Create prompt flow*

You can create a new prompt flow by using samples available from the portal or by creating a new prompt. Once you click the **Create** button, the prompt flow authoring page opens, as shown in Figure 3-3.

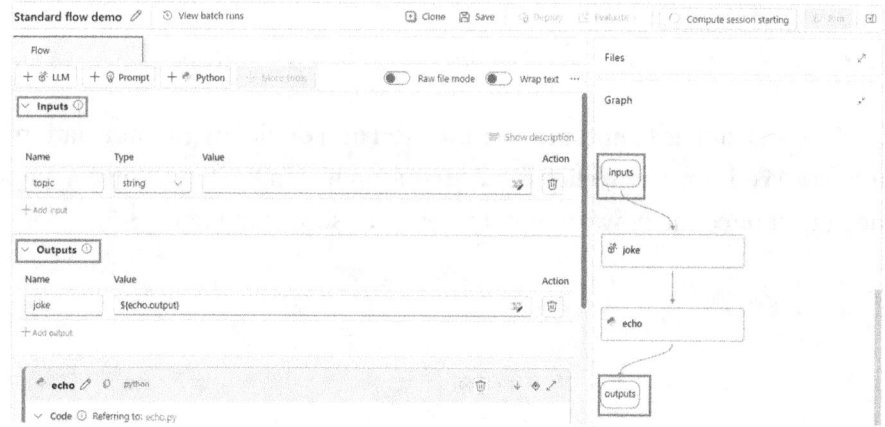

Figure 3-3. *Prompt flow authoring page*

63

CHAPTER 3   BUILDING WITH PROMPT FLOW

Click the **Compute session starting** button on the prompt flow authoring page, as shown in Figure 3-3, to define your prompt flow. By default, the sample prompt flow is open. You see the visualization flow on the right side, which is just a pictorial representation to describe your flow; you can't edit it. You can add more tool options from the top of the page using LLM, Prompt, or Python. Or, click **More tools** to do the same (see Figure 3-4). In the input section, you can add values for your topic (e.g., "space").

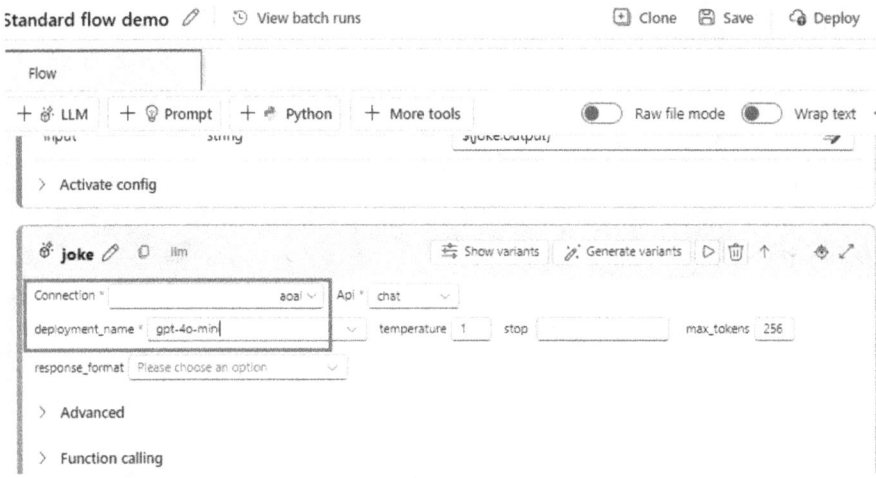

Figure 3-4. *Connection and deployment in LLM editor*

The next step is to enter the connection and deployment information in the LLM editor. Then, click the **Run** button to run the flow. You can view the output once the flow run is completed, as shown in Figure 3-5.

64

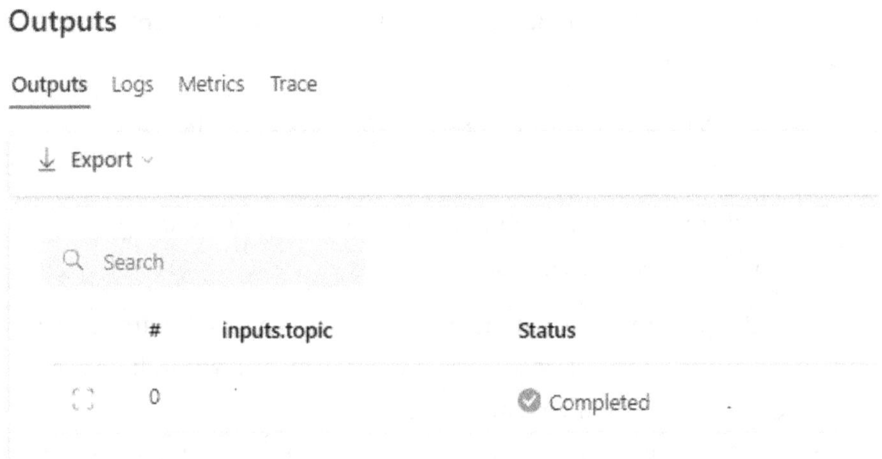

Outputs

#	inputs.topic	Status
0		✓ Completed

Figure 3-5. *Prompt flow output*

So using the prompt flow, you can create reusable small components that enhance collaboration and LLMops integration. Let's discuss the importance of AI Foundry prompt flow with a very simple example.

Imagine a company that wants to use Azure OpenAI to automate responses to customer inquiries. Without prompt flows, developers must manually execute the following tasks.

1. Write complex scripts to call the LLM API.
2. Test prompts iteratively to refine accuracy.
3. Use external data sources for personalized responses.
4. Deploy and monitor the system manually.

But for this use case, the prompt flow allows you to define and execute a simple flow as often as you want. With prompt flow, you can do the following.

- Design visual workflows: Step-by-step flows connecting LLMs, APIs, and databases.

CHAPTER 3   BUILDING WITH PROMPT FLOW

- Automated validation and testing: Compare different prompt variations.

- Performance optimization: Improve accuracy, latency, and costs.

- Ease of deployment: Integrate with applications using built-in deployment tools.

To run the prompt flow, you need a compute session. Environment settings for compute resources are defined in **flow.dag.yaml**. It uses a serverless compute with a virtual machine.

To start the compute session, go to the AI Foundry portal, select **Prompt flow** in the left pane, select the prompt flow you want to execute, and click **Start compute session** as highlighted in Figure 3-6.

Figure 3-6. *Start compute session for prompt flow*

To customize the advanced settings, click **Start with advanced settings** (see Figure 3-7).

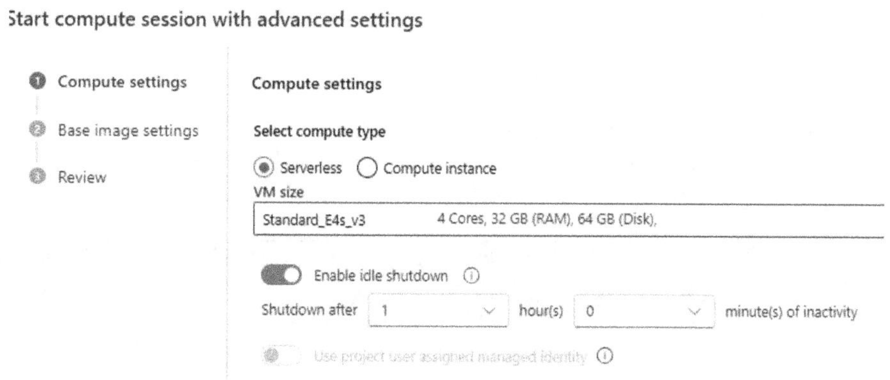

CHAPTER 3 BUILDING WITH PROMPT FLOW

Start compute session with advanced settings

① Compute settings	Compute settings
② Base image settings	Select compute type
③ Review	● Serverless ○ Compute instance

VM size

Standard_E4s_v3   4 Cores, 32 GB (RAM), 64 GB (Disk),

Enable idle shutdown

Shutdown after 1   hour(s) 0   minute(s) of inactivity

Use project user assigned managed identity

Figure 3-7. *Serverless compute configuration for prompt flow compute*

Table 3-1. *Compute Choices for Prompt Flow*

Serverless Compute	**Compute Instance**
Adjust virtual machine size	Fix the virtual machine size
Set idle time to save cost when it is not in use	Set idle time to save cost
Use a user-managed identity to install packages	Use the default user-managed identity

As you can see in Figure 3-8, when you use a compute instance after selecting the compute instance, you can click **Next** to choose the image setting. After selecting the image, click **Next** to review and apply, **and start compute session**.

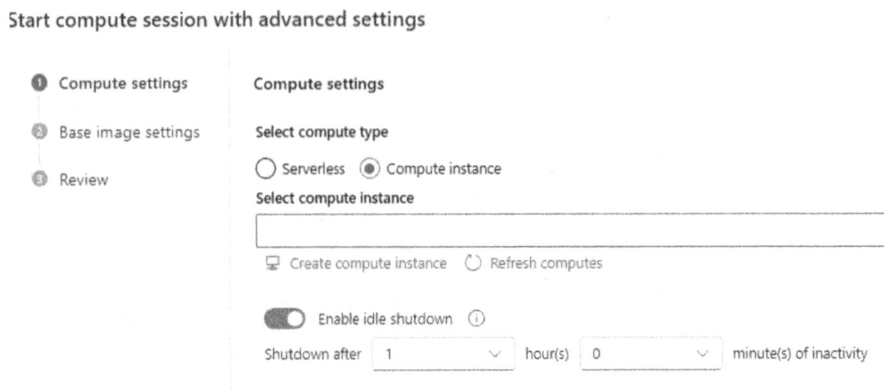

CHAPTER 3   BUILDING WITH PROMPT FLOW

Start compute session with advanced settings

Figure 3-8. Compute instance for prompt flow

You can do multiple configuration changes to compute sessions using the top toolbar of the prompt flow page, as highlighted in Figure 3-9.

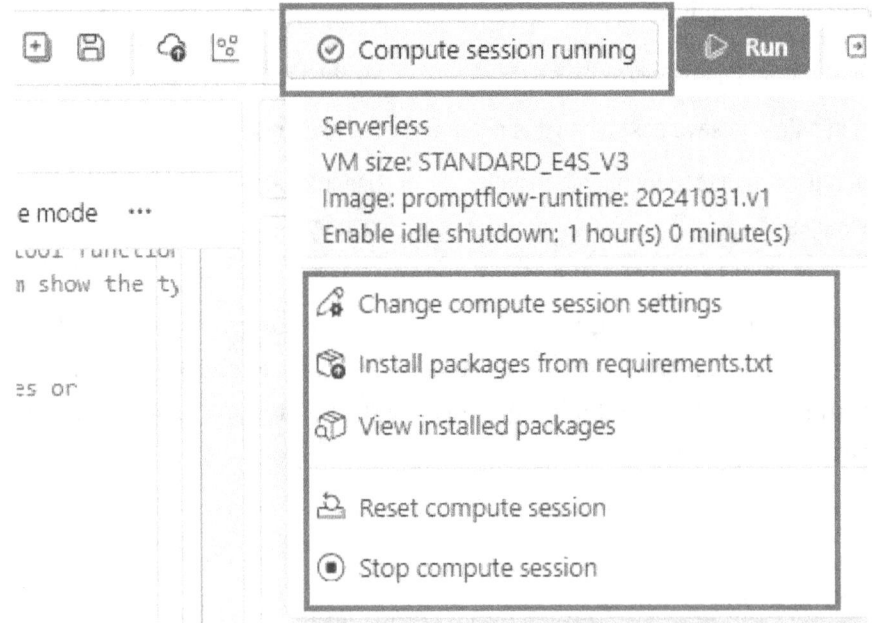

Figure 3-9. Change compute session configurations

CHAPTER 3   BUILDING WITH PROMPT FLOW

- Change the compute session setting
- Install packages from requirements.txt
- View installed packages
- Reset compute session
- Stop the compute session

To change the compute environment of your prompt flow, you can add more packages to the requirements.txt file. After updating the packages in the requirements.txt file, you can do the following to change your environment (see Figure 3-10).

- **Save and install**: Execute the **pip install -r requirements.txt** command.

- **Save only**: Save the requirements.txt file and install the packages later.

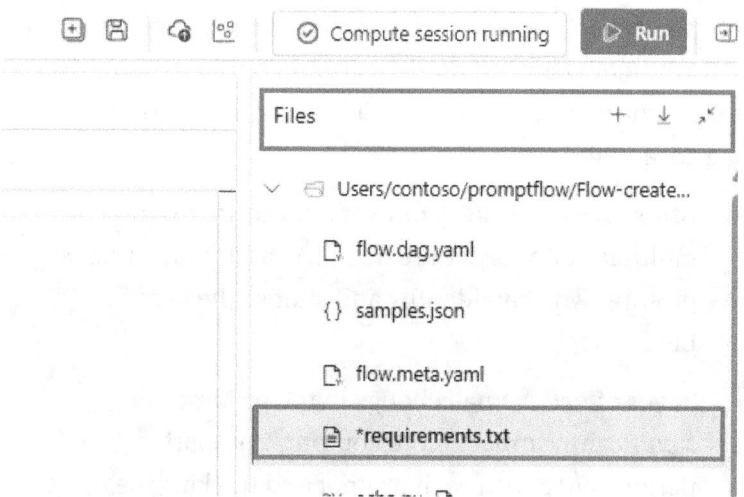

Figure 3-10. *Change requirements.txt file*

CHAPTER 3 BUILDING WITH PROMPT FLOW

A basic image is used by default, but you can change the image by opening the prompt flow, selecting **Raw file mode** from the top toolbar to enable editing, and selecting **flow.dag.yaml** in the Files section, as shown in Figure 3-11.

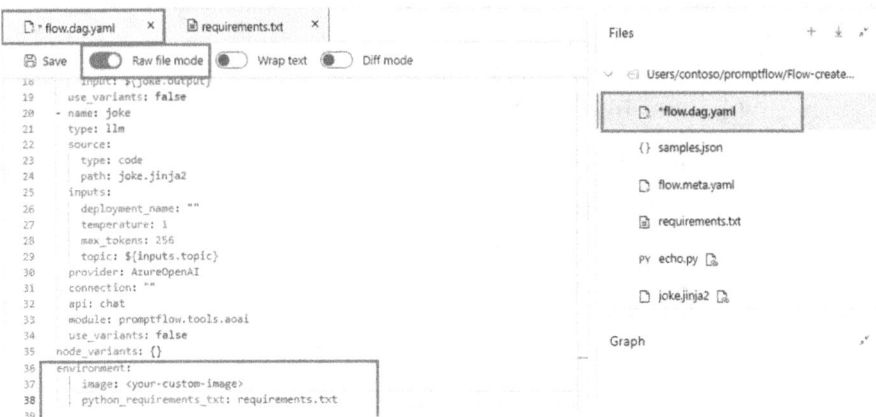

Figure 3-11. Edit flow.dag.yaml file

In the environment section, you can specify the image name. Creating a prompt is not a simple task; it can also be challenging. Variants can validate the model's behavior under various conditions, such as context, temperature, formatting, or top-k. Using variants for prompt flow has the following advantages.

- **Improves the quality of LLM generation**: With multiple variants of the same LLM node with various prompts, you can identify and choose the best LLM model.

- **Saves effort**: A small change in the prompt can significantly impact model output. Comparing performance with each prompt and tracking the historical versions saves a lot of time before moving to production and doing tuning later on.

CHAPTER 3 BUILDING WITH PROMPT FLOW

- **Enhances productivity**: Streamline LLM models with multiple variants with improved results and less time, which improves overall productivity.

Understanding the Copilot Stack

While developing and building AI models and generative AI applications, it is very critical to understand the complete technology stack. Using the Microsoft Copilot stack, you can simplify and enhance the building of custom agents. It provides a visual guide with an intelligent and natural language-driven experience powered by LLMs. Microsoft Copilot enhances and accelerates overall GenAI application building. It is an AI-powered assistant that helps users with tasks across Microsoft products like Word, Excel, PowerPoint, Outlook, Teams, and more. It uses advanced AI models, including OpenAI's GPT-4, to generate content, summarize information, analyze data, and automate repetitive work as seen in Figure 3-12.

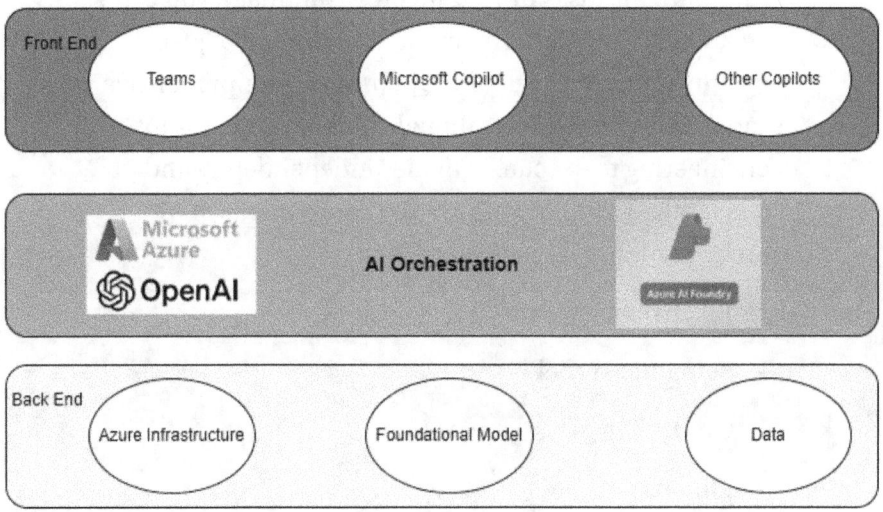

Figure 3-12. *Microsoft Copilot stack*

CHAPTER 3   BUILDING WITH PROMPT FLOW

The Microsoft Copilot stack mainly consists of three layers.

- **Back end**: The back-end layer mainly consists of the infrastructure where the large language model is deployed and customizes this model based on your data, so end users get the right domain-specific response to their questions. Azure OpenAI Service enables GPT language models, backed by Microsoft Azure's AI services and infrastructure, with security, compliance, and responsible AI content filtering. Selecting Azure OpenAI and Azure for your Copilot stack's back-end sets a solid foundation for supporting your AI model development.

- **AI orchestration**: It is the backbone of the Copilot stack. With AI orchestration, it is easier to manage AI components and services with your custom AI agent to execute complex tasks. For example, when summarizing tasks in your meeting summary, you can create follow-up tasks on command instead of just creating a summary. Azure OpenAI has comprehensive capabilities like conversational chatbots and prompt engineering to execute activities independently and efficiently. The following are key components of AI orchestration.

    – Business logic

    – Semantic kernel

    – Grounding

    – Plugins

- **User experience layer**: The front-end layer mainly consists of a user interface that allows end users to interact with apps like Microsoft 365. Unlike traditional user interfaces like buttons/screens, Copilot focuses on conversational design. The following are key components of user experience layers.

  - Conversational design
  - Meta prompts
  - Coherence with conversation
  - Accessibility and interaction with groups

To cater to your business needs, you can extend Microsoft Copilot capabilities to develop your own custom agent. You can add instructions, actions, and knowledge while customizing your application with Microsoft Copilot, as mentioned in Figure 3-13.

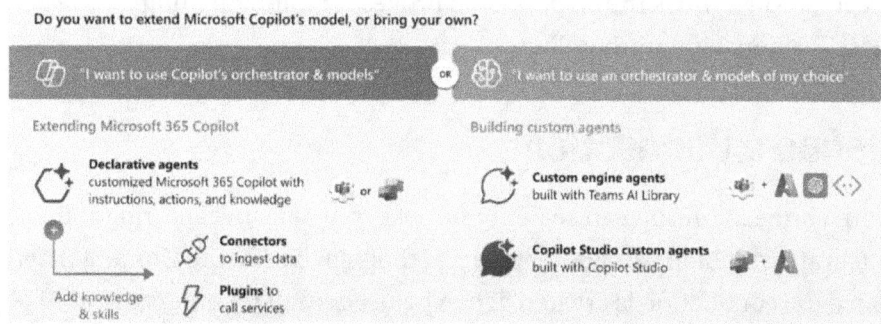

Figure 3-13. Customize Microsoft Copilot for your application

There are two options for building a custom agent.

- **Extend Microsoft 365 Copilot**: Customize Microsoft Copilot with declarative agents for improved collaboration, productivity, and workflow with a consistent, personalized experience, and automate complex processes.

73

- **Build custom agents**: You can use Azure OpenAI and Teams AI Library to provide comprehensive tools for developing your copilot.

AI Foundry prompt flow sits in the AI orchestration layer of Copilot Studio. A prompt flow uses all the underlying Azure infrastructure. With prompt flow, you can develop small packets of complex AI systems that can be reused many times. It is capable of making use of all deployed generative AI applications. Microsoft Copilot is an emerging, powerful framework for developing business AI-driven solutions.

Web Classification Using Prompt Flow

Let's start building your first prompt flow, which classifies web URLs into various categories. To start, first go to the Azure portal using `https://portal.azure.com` and go to the resource where AI Foundry is created. Now, check the step-by-step process of implementing the web classification with prompt flow.

Define a Connection

With connection, you can securely store keys or sensitive information to integrate with LLMs and other external tools such as Azure Content Safety. Once the connection is created, it can be used by all members of the AI Foundry project. To check if the Azure OpenAI connection exists, click the prompt flow and select the **Connections** tab, as shown in Figure 3-14. If there is already a connection for Azure OpenAI, you can skip the setup process.

CHAPTER 3 BUILDING WITH PROMPT FLOW

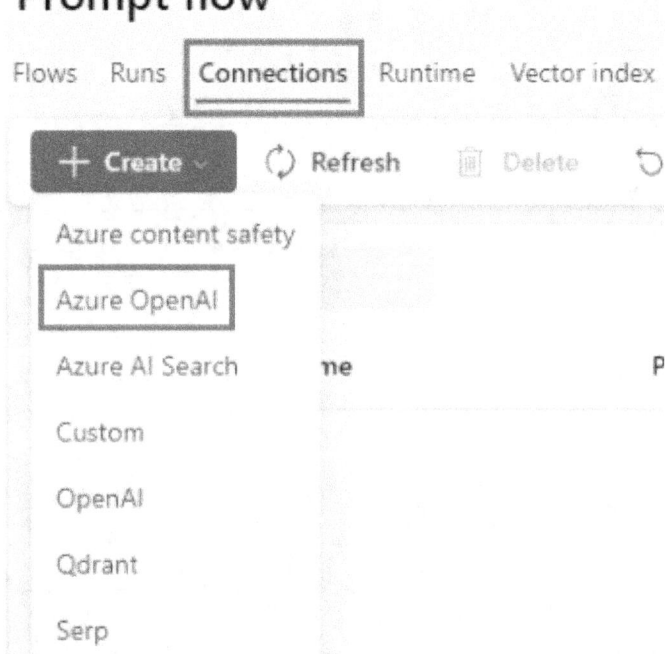

Figure 3-14. Connection in AI Foundry prompt flow

But if the Azure OpenAI connection is not present, select **Create** and **Azure OpenAI** from the drop-down. Once the dialog box appears, configure all required details (e.g., name, providers, subscription ID, Azure OpenAI account names, etc.), as highlighted in Figure 3-15.

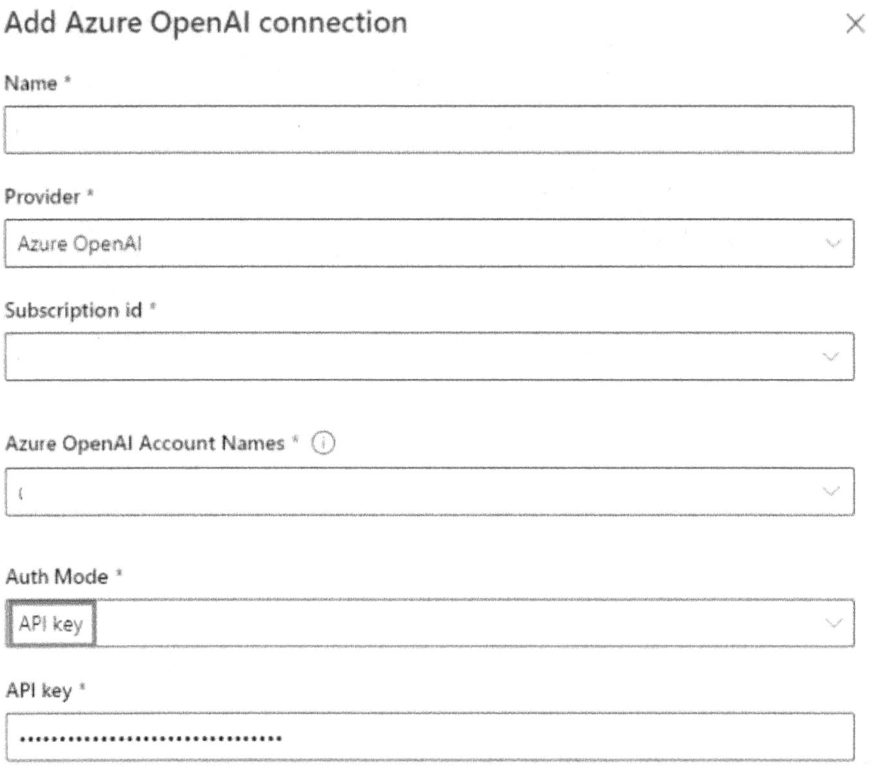

CHAPTER 3   BUILDING WITH PROMPT FLOW

Figure 3-15. Add Azure OpenAI connection

To gather the API information, go to the chat playground in the Azure OpenAI portal and select your OpenAI resource name. You can copy and use the key in the API Key field, as Figure 3-16 highlights.

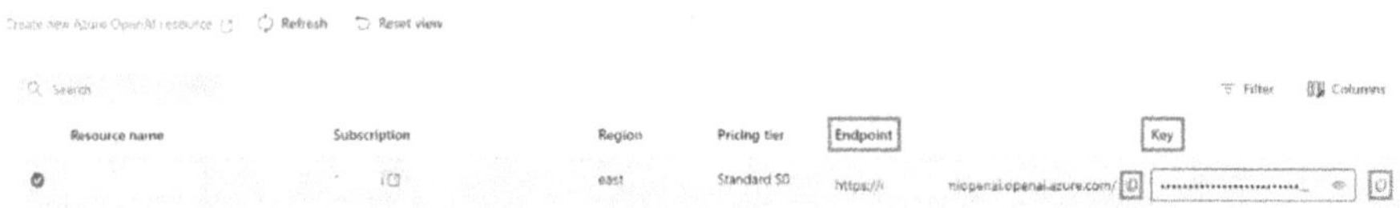

Figure 3-16. API key from AI Foundry chat playground

CHAPTER 3 BUILDING WITH PROMPT FLOW

After entering all the details, select **Save** to create the connection. Once a connection is created, you can link it with the deployment before you run the LLM nodes in the prompt flow.

Develop a Prompt Flow

Go to the prompt flow home page and select **Create** to create a prompt flow. You can browse the built-in samples from the **Explore gallery** tab and click **View detail** to learn more about the sample flow (see Figure 3-17).

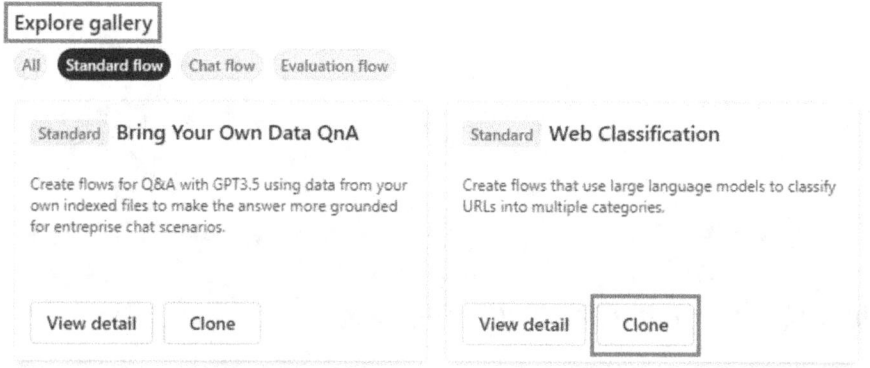

Figure 3-17. *Explore gallery*

Let's use the web classification samples from the prompt flow page for our use case for web classification. Web classification is a prompt flow with multiclass classification with LLM. The URL is an input that classifies the URL into a web category. For example, if the input URL is https://www.facebook.com/, then it classifies the URL as a social media website. To clone this web classification sample, click the **Clone** button. You can see the location to save the flow within the workspace. Use the **Edit** button to edit the prompt flow.

CHAPTER 3   BUILDING WITH PROMPT FLOW

Start a Compute Session

To execute a prompt flow, click **Start compute session**, as highlighted in Figure 3-18.

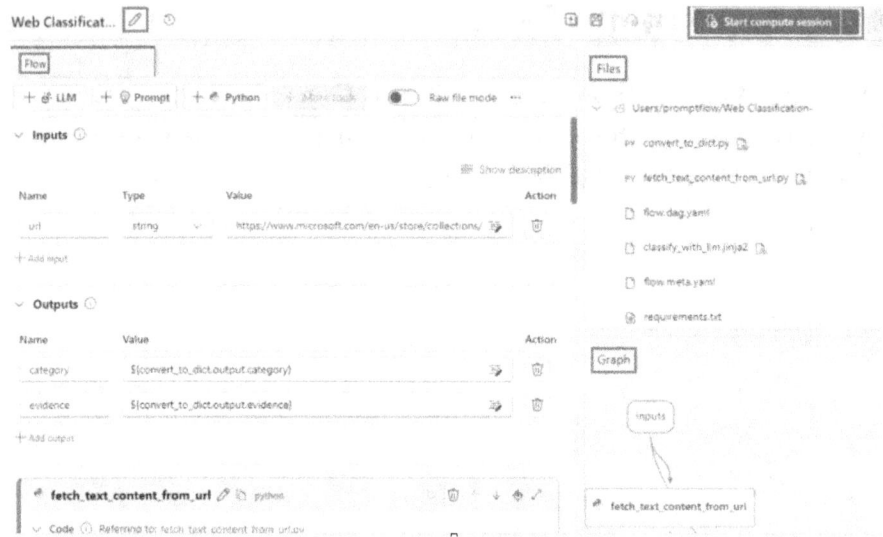

Figure 3-18. *Prompt flow authoring page*

Click **Start compute session** on the prompt flow authoring page to execute the prompt flow. The prompt flow authoring page is divided into three main components.

- **Flow**: The main working area where you can author the flow by adding, removing, and improving your prompt flow. You can edit inputs and outputs.

- **Files**: On the top right side of your prompt authoring page, you can see the file and folder structure of the prompt flow. You can create, add, and remove files for development, testing, and collaboration.

78

CHAPTER 3 BUILDING WITH PROMPT FLOW

- **Visual graphs**: The lower right side has a visual representation of the graph, which you can zoom in or out of to see the overall flow of the prompt. As shown in Figure 3-19, you can edit the files from the files section or enable raw file mode from the top of the toolbar.

Figure 3-19. Raw file mode in prompt flow

In our example prompt flow, the URL is the input to the flow. It uses a Python script to get the text content from the URL and provide input to the LLM model. It uses LLM to summarize text content. It classifies based on the URL and the summarized content from the LLM model. Here, the Python script converts the LLM output to a dictionary.

Set up LLM Nodes

Use the connection for each LLM node to set up LLM API keys, and depending on the connection type, select the deployment name as highlighted in Figure 3-20.

79

CHAPTER 3 BUILDING WITH PROMPT FLOW

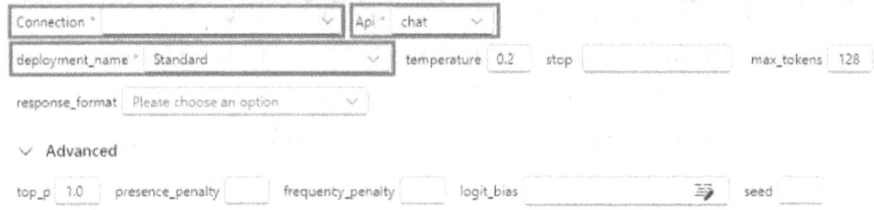

Figure 3-20. Connection and deployment setup for prompt flow

Once the Prompt Flow Is Ready

Once the prompt flow is ready, you can run the flow by clicking the **Run** button and **View outputs**, as highlighted in Figure 3-21.

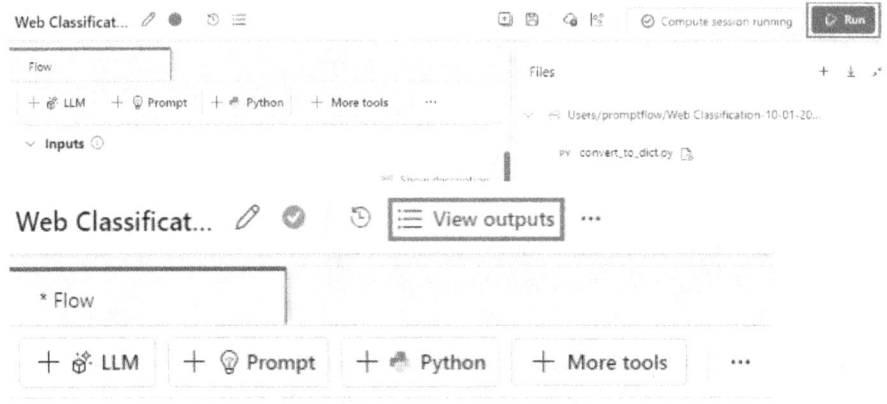

Figure 3-21. Execute prompt flow

You can use the Batch run & Evaluate option to configure and submit a batch run to evaluate a prompt flow. The evaluation methods use Python or LLM to validate the accuracy and efficiency of the model. Select **Evaluate** from the top of the prompt authoring page and configure **Basic settings ➤ Batch run settings**, as highlighted in Figure 3-22.

80

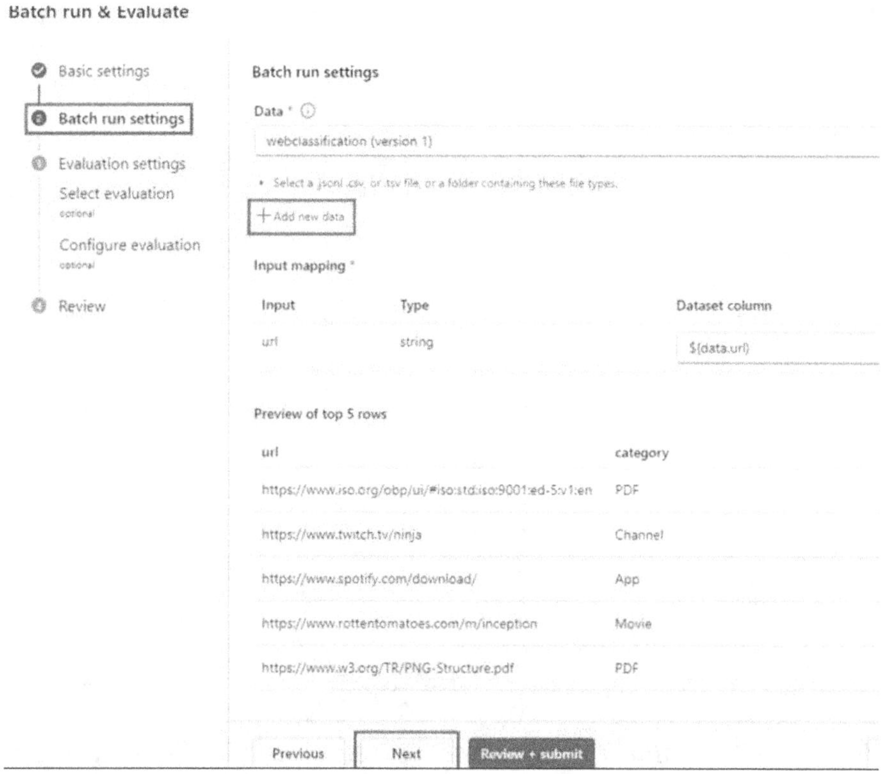

CHAPTER 3   BUILDING WITH PROMPT FLOW

Figure 3-22.   Batch run and evaluate prompt flow

Click the **Next** button to enter the **Evaluation settings** details. This page shows built-in and customized evaluation flows. In our use case, web classification is a classification scenario, so you must select **Classification Selection Accuracy** for evaluation, and then select **Next**. On the **Configuration evaluation** page, enter the details **under Evaluation input mapping**. Specify groundtruth as **${data.category}** and prediction as **${run.outputs.category}**, as highlighted in Figure 3-23.

CHAPTER 3 BUILDING WITH PROMPT FLOW

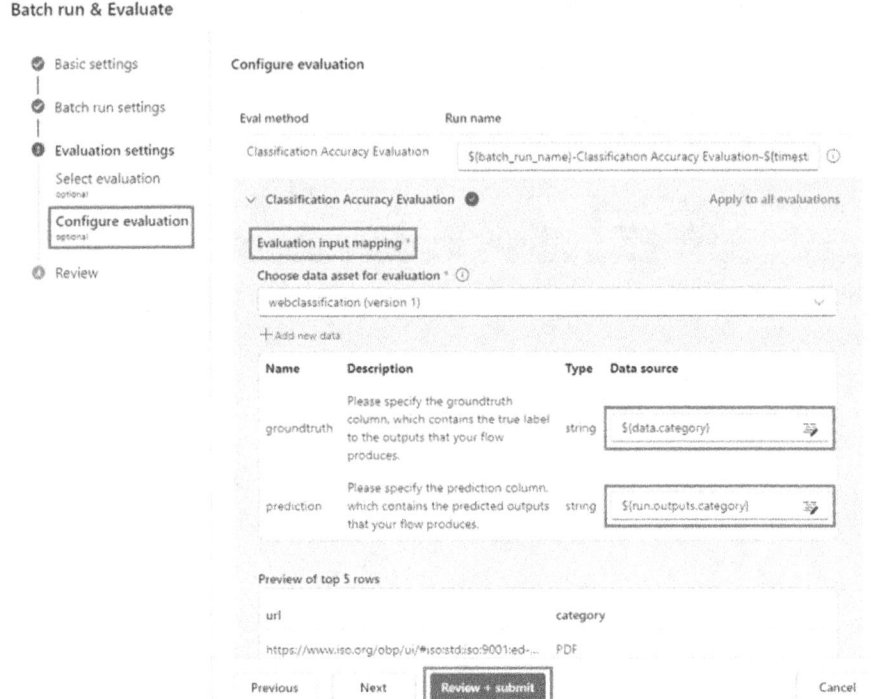

Figure 3-23. *Evaluation settings: Select evaluation + Configure evaluation*

The next step is to review, submit the batch run, and check the results. You can view the run status in the View Run List. You can see the following metrics in the **Visualize outputs** section, as highlighted in Figure 3-24.

- Token count
- Accuracy
- Result: Correct or Incorrect

CHAPTER 3 BUILDING WITH PROMPT FLOW

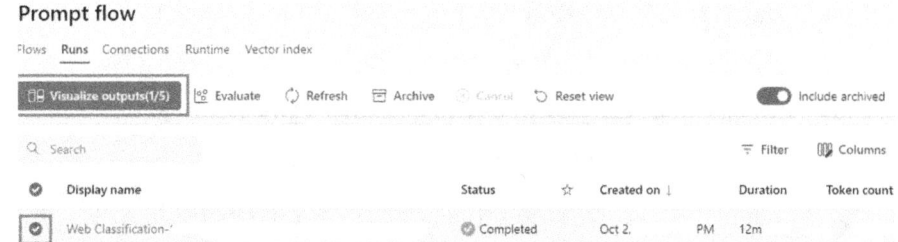

Figure 3-24. *Visualize output for prompt flow*

After building and successfully testing the flow, you can deploy the model as an endpoint by selecting the **Deploy** button from the top of the menu bar.

Integrating External APIs with AI Foundry

Integrating external APIs with Azure AI Foundry improves overall development and efficiency of the AI model by enabling it to access real-time data and extending the functionality beyond the built-in model. Azure AI Foundry supports external API integration through Microsoft prompt flows, function calling, and custom connectors. These allow AI models to fetch external data, process responses dynamically, and perform specific actions based on API calls.

You need the following to integrate external APIs within the Azure AI Foundry prompt flow.

- **Azure AI Studio and AI Foundry set up**: Ensure you have access to Azure AI Studio and have set up AI Foundry.

- **API key and authentication**: APIs often require authentication via API keys, OAuth, or other methods.

- **Prompt flow connector**: Use the API node in prompt flow to connect external APIs and fetch real-time data.

- **Data transformation layer**: Process API responses to structure them for AI consumption.

- **Security and compliance**: Handle API data securely, ensuring compliance with enterprise policies.

Let's review the step-by-step process of integrating external APIs with Azure AI Foundry.

1. Choose the right API.

    a. Check whether the API is REST, SOAP, or GraphQL.

    b. Validate authentication requirements.

    c. Review rate limits and response format.

2. Configure the API call in a prompt flow.

    a. Use the functional calling feature in the prompt flow to define an API request.

    b. Use Python or Power Automate to handle advanced API integration.

3. Execute API calls in AI Foundry.

    a. Use **requests** in Python in JavaScript to call APIs.

    b. Structure API response to process them efficiently with AI models.

The following example calls the external weather API in Azure AI Foundry.

```
import requests
import json

def get_weather(city: str) -> dict:
    """
    Get real-time weather data from OpenWeatherMap API.
```

```python
    """
    API_KEY = "your_api_key_here"
    BASE_URL = "https://api.openweathermap.org/data/2.5/weather"

    params = {
        "q": city,
        "appid": API_KEY,
        "units": "metric"
    }

    try:
        response = requests.get(BASE_URL, params=params)
        data = response.json()

        if response.status_code == 200:
            weather_info = {
                "City": data["name"],
                "Temperature": f"{data['main']['temp']}°C",
                "Condition": data["weather"][0]["description"],
                "Humidity": f"{data['main']['humidity']}%",
                "Wind Speed": f"{data['wind']['speed']} m/s"
            }
            return weather_info
        else:
            return {"Error": data.get("message", "Failed to fetch weather data")}

    except Exception as e:
        return {"Error": str(e)}
```

CHAPTER 3 BUILDING WITH PROMPT FLOW

4. Integrate AI models.

   a. Use Azure AI functions to call APIs.

   b. Pass API responses as input parameters to LLMs.

   c. Use retrieval-augmented generation to fetch data for AI-generated insights.

5. Secure and optimize API calls.

   a. Secure API requests.

   b. Implement caching for frequently accessed APIs.

   c. Monitor rate limits.

Function Calling and Advanced Workflows

Function calling allows LLMs to call external APIs, databases, or functions to get real-time data and perform structured tasks. This feature enhances the model's capabilities beyond static responses, enabling dynamic interactions with external systems.

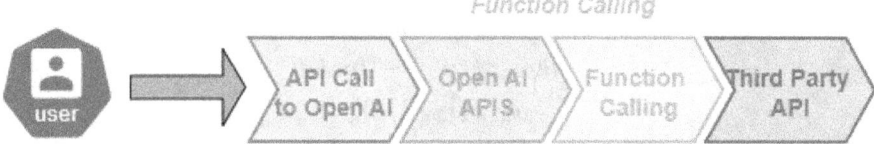

Figure 3-25. Function calling in OpenAI

The latest versions of gpt-35 and gpt-4 can work with functions. During the function call in OpenAI, when one or more functions are included in the request, the model determines which function to call based on the prompt context. Model creates an API call and generates output data based on the functions you call. The following are the high-level steps of calling functions with the OpenAI model, which are highlighted in Figure 3-25.

CHAPTER 3   BUILDING WITH PROMPT FLOW

1. Trigger the chat completion APIs with your function based on the user input.

2. Call the API or function based on the model response.

3. Complete the chat completions API again based on the response from the function to get output.

Although function calling capability can be used in LLMs, it is wisely used for the following reasons. Know the potential risks and measures to use it wisely.

- **Evaluate function calls.** Validate the function calls created from your model with various parameters, based on which function is called, and also ensure it is based on the user's request.

- **Use trusted data.** It is only recommended that trusted and reliable data be used. Use of unauthorized data can impact the overall output of your model.

- **Follow the principle of least privilege access.** It only provides the least access necessary to your function, which should be called in your model. For example, when you are using function calls to query a database, the function should only have read-only access to the database and not provide more access.

- **Validate real-world impacts.** When you execute the function calls from your models, make sure you validate the real-world impact to avoid any risks or potential impact.

- **Implement user confirmations.** To save time and cost, add user confirmations so the end user can validate and provide input before the model generates the output.

Conclusion

Microsoft prompt flows provide a powerful and structured approach to developing AI-powered applications, enabling seamless interaction between LLMs and external systems. This chapter explored the foundational aspects of prompt flow, from creating simple I/O flows in AI Studio to understanding the Copilot stack and implementing web classification models. Additionally, you examined how to integrate external APIs and leverage function calling for advanced workflows, showcasing how prompt flow can be adapted to complex business use cases.

By mastering these techniques, developers and architects can design more efficient, scalable, and intelligent AI applications that integrate seamlessly into enterprise ecosystems. As AI adoption grows, leveraging prompt flow will accelerate development, improve automation, and ensure AI-driven solutions deliver maximum value. The following chapters dive deeper into optimizing AI workflows, ensuring responsible AI practices, and deploying robust AI solutions within Microsoft's ecosystem.

CHAPTER 4

Bringing Your Own Data to AI Foundry

The previous chapter covered the powerful capabilities of a Microsoft prompt flow within Azure AI Foundry. From creating simple input/output flows to building advanced workflows with the Copilot stack, you saw how developers can orchestrate large language model (LLM) operations, integrate external APIs, and implement function calling for more complex interactions. This foundation gave us a glimpse into the potential of prompt engineering and modular flow design in real-world AI applications.

Now, let's shift our focus to an essential capability that significantly enhances the contextual relevance and accuracy of LLM responses: retrieval-augmented generation.

By the end of this chapter, you'll be able to leverage your own data securely and efficiently within generative AI workflows—transforming static LLMs into dynamic, knowledge-aware copilots.

This chapter covers the following topics.

- An introduction to retrieval-augmented generation
- Setting up a retrieval-augmented generation infrastructure and prompt flows
- Connecting and managing data stores for LLMs

CHAPTER 4   BRINGING YOUR OWN DATA TO AI FOUNDRY

Introduction to Retrieval-Augmented Generation

AI technologies have become very important in today's fast-paced world. In the early days of the software world, rule-based systems were built, followed by advanced neural networks, where each step is expanded with what AI can do with the language. Major development in this journey is the introduction of retrieval-augmented generation (RAG). It is a powerful pattern in modern AI that combines traditional information retrieval with generative models like GPT to produce more accurate and context-rich responses.

While LLMs are powerful, they are often limited by the data they were trained on and their inability to access up-to-date or domain-specific information. RAG addresses this limitation by enabling LLMs to fetch relevant information from custom data sources at runtime, making responses more grounded, accurate, and trustworthy.

Let's break down RAG using a practical example.

Suppose you're building an AI assistant for a bank's internal knowledge base. The assistant should answer employee questions like the following.

> "What is the process to escalate a loan approval that has been delayed?"

If you only use a standard GPT model (without RAG), it might misunderstand the question and provide an erroneous answer.

🔍 R: Retrieval

It retrieves relevant documents or data from an external source based on the user's query.

In our example, the system retrieves PDF documents or documents containing the bank's standard operating procedures (SOPs) about loan processing.

✳ A: Augmentation

The retrieved documents are augmented into the prompt passed to the LLM. This gives the model real context.

In our example, the model's prompt is now as follows.

> "Given the following document excerpt:
>
> 'To escalate a loan approval that has been delayed, notify the regional manager via email and log the request in CRM with a delay reason code'
>
> Answer the user's question."

 G: Generation

The language model now generates a human-like response using the augmented context.

The following is from our example.

> "To escalate a loan approval that has been delayed, notify the regional manager via email and log the delay in the CRM with the appropriate reason code. Refer to SOP-345 for complete steps."

RAG is an approach that combines a large language model with external data sources. Using the external dataset as per the context improves the LLM response by getting relevant information from the external dataset to get a more accurate output with the context of the provided dataset. It is similar to how humans make decisions. To make decisions, the human brain tries to compare current situations with past situations and make decisions accordingly. While working with generative AI models, if you don't use RAG, the response you get may be outdated or hallucinated, which can significantly impact the output's accuracy.

A good example of RAG in a production-scale product is what perplexity has achieved. It is a search engine that uses RAG to improve the search results by grounding them in live online searches. It provides accurate and up-to-date information to the user's response.

Figure 4-1 shows how the classical RAG workflow works.

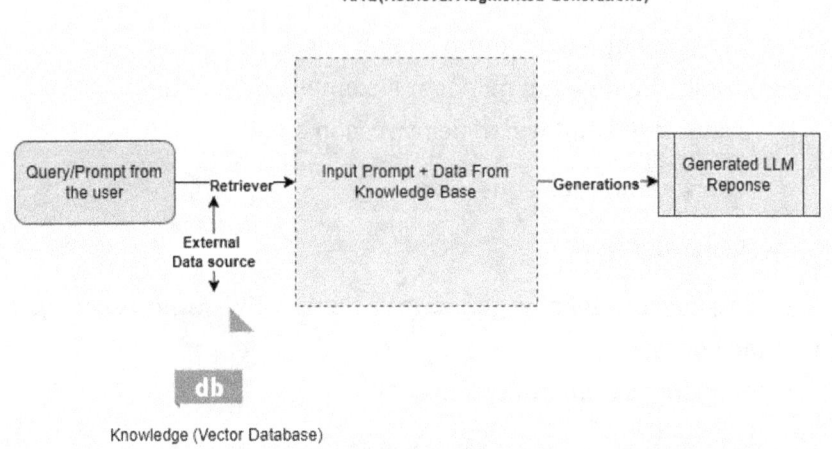

Figure 4-1. Classic RAG

A classic RAG workflow has three primary phases. After the input prompt from the end user, the LLM gathers knowledge from the static training data, which consists of a large number of documents/texts.

In the augmentation phase, it uses vector databases, also known as a knowledge base, that have external data that can be used to set up contextual knowledge to provide an accurate response to the input prompt. In natural language processing and RAG, text information is transformed into numerical presentations called vectors to capture the semantic information. A vector represents words or statements to maintain the key properties of the text. Storing text in the form of numbers improves the overall efficiency of finding the relevant document or content to provide prompt output to the end user.

The generator in the LLM model generates the output to the prompt and gives it to the end user.

In a nutshell, when the user asks the end user questions, the following process happens.

1. **Retrieval**: Retrievers access the vector database to find the relevant information or contextual knowledge for the user prompt.

2. **Augmentation**: The augmentation process builds the contextual knowledge based on the information received via the retrieval process to prepare accurate results for the user prompt.

3. **Generation**: Contextual information received by the user prompt in the augmentation process generates output and shares it with the end user.

The following are the fundamentals of the RAG process.

- **External knowledge/data Integration**: The main difference between traditional LLM and RAG-based LLM is that the generic LLM model is trained only on the data available on the Internet. However, the RAG-based LLM model integrates external data sources to create more contextual and accurate output for the user prompt.

- **Dynamic information retrieval**: RAG process automatically fetches relevant data dynamically from the knowledge base or vector databases to find the contextual information.

- **Contextual response to user prompt**: Using the contextual knowledge, find the contextual data to craft more accurate and context-aware answers.

Table 4-1 highlights the differences between a traditional LLM and RAG.

Table 4-1. Traditional LLM vs. RAG

Traditional LLM	RAG
The knowledge source is static.	Knowledge source is dynamic. It uses an external knowledge base.
Retraining is required to update the knowledge.	It uses data dynamically in real time.
Model size is limited.	It combines retrieval to extend the context.
There is a greater possibility of inaccuracies due to non-contextual data.	There is highly accurate data with contextual knowledge.
It is expensive to train LLMs.	It is less expensive due to enabling data in an external database.
The complexity of the setup is low.	The complexity of the setup is high.
Information/data used can be outdated.	Information/data used is up-to-date.
There is limited support for business-specific data.	It is easier to integrate with external data for business-specific use cases.

Setting up a RAG Infrastructure and Prompt Flows

In the Azure AI Foundry portal, Azure AI Search is an enterprise-ready information retrieval service to enable/upload external data sources to implement RAG. Before setting up the prompt flow to implement RAG, let's look at its architecture, as illustrated in Figure 4-2.

CHAPTER 4 BRINGING YOUR OWN DATA TO AI FOUNDRY

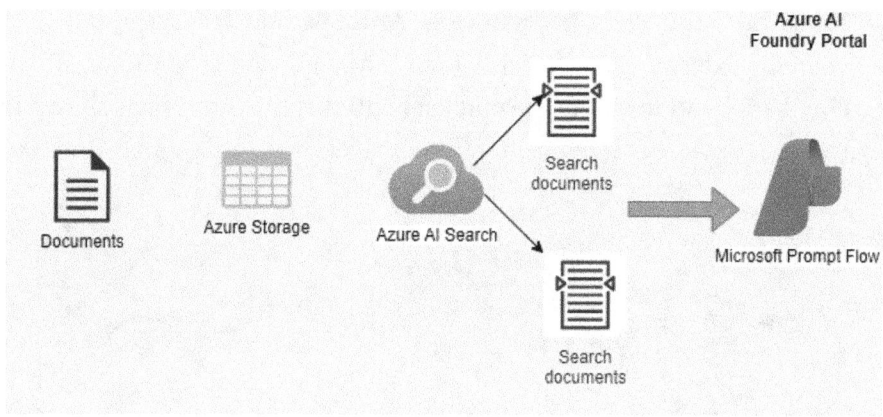

Figure 4-2. *Prompt flow RAG architecture in AI Foundry*

To implement the RAG, you must have external datasets, databases, or knowledge bases that you want to feed to the LLM model. You can put those knowledge bases or documents in an Azure storage account. Once all the context-related information is in Azure Storage, you can link it to the Azure AI Search service. The key thing to note here is that you can use structured and unstructured data. From the RAG architecture point of view, the retrieval process happens here from the Azure storage account to the Azure AI Search service. With Azure AI Search, you can build RAG- and A2A-based (agent to agent) applications on Azure with native LLM integration.

Azure AI Search can be used in both traditional and generative scenarios. Azure AI Search service has the following capabilities.

- An efficient search engine with rich indexing capabilities
- Supports lexical analysis for text and optional applied AI
- Scalability, security, and integration with Azure services without the physical transfer of data

CHAPTER 4   BRINGING YOUR OWN DATA TO AI FOUNDRY

From the architecture point of view, Azure AI Search service sits between the external data source, which is not indexed or raw data, and the client application where the end user submits the prompt, as shown in Figure 4-3.

Figure 4-3.* Azure AI Search position in the Azure architecture*

Inside the Azure AI Search service, two primary workloads are indexing and querying.

- **Indexing**: With indexing, it loads the content from the external data available from the Azure service to the AI search service. Internally, the content or data is processed in the form of tokens and stored in indexes. The format in which AI search stores data is in JSON format. With cognitive search, which supports skills for optical character recognition (OCR), key phrase extraction, language detection, and so forth, you can also use image or language models.

- **Querying**: Once the indexing is populated with the searchable content, you can query the relevant data when the client application sends the requests via prompt. Semantic ranking is an extension of query execution that adds secondary ranks using natural language to revalidate and evaluate result sets and find relevant contextual results.

CHAPTER 4   BRINGING YOUR OWN DATA TO AI FOUNDRY

Setting up a RAG infrastructure and integrating it with a prompt flow in Azure AI Foundry (via Azure AI Studio) is key to building powerful, contextual, and enterprise-grade AI solutions.

Let's go through the step-by-step process of how to set up the RAG infrastructure and prompt flow in Azure AI Foundry.

Step 1: Set up RAG Infrastructure in AI Foundry
Prepare Your Data

Ensure your unstructured data (PDFs, Word docs, websites, etc.) is available in one of the supported formats. Data can be stored in Azure Blob Storage, Azure Data Lake, or SharePoint.

Create a Search Optimized Vector Index

Azure AI Studio allows you to create a vector index using the following.

- Azure AI Search (for hybrid search: keyword + vector)
- Azure AI Search vector index (pure vector-based RAG)

Go to the Azure AI Foundry portal and select **Project overview ➤ Settings**, as highlighted in Figure 4-4.

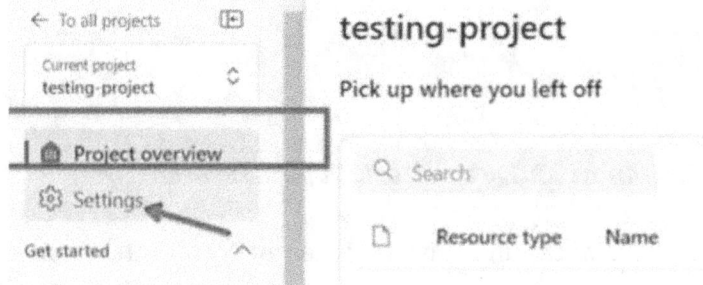

Figure 4-4. *Azure AI Foundry project settings*

CHAPTER 4   BRINGING YOUR OWN DATA TO AI FOUNDRY

Next, click **New connection** from the right pane and select the **Azure Blob Storage**, as shown in Figure 4-5.

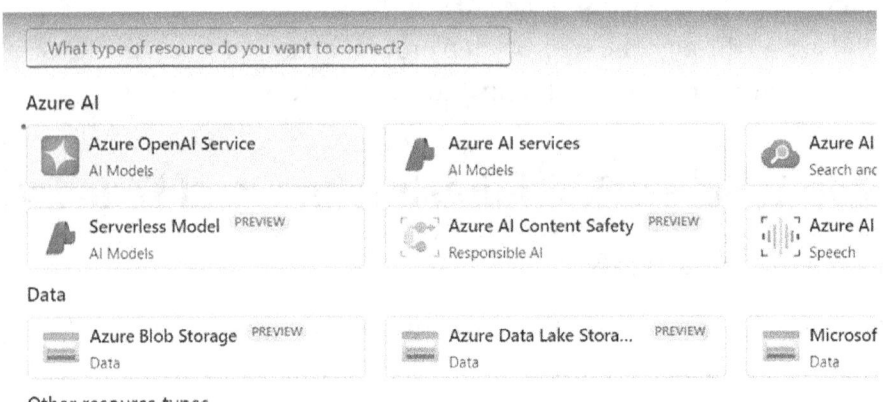

Figure 4-5. AI Foundry connection

Use the **Index this data** option to create, as highlighted in Figure 4-6.

- Document chunking

- Embedding generation using `text-embedding-ada-002` (OpenAI model) or custom models

- Index storage (usually cognitive search)

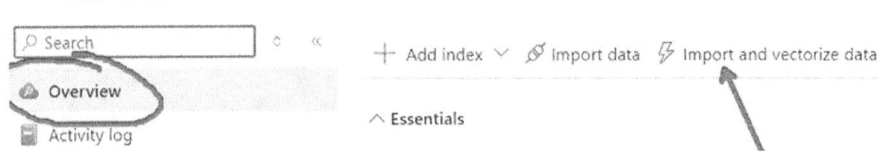

Figure 4-6. Import and vectorize data for AI search

Now this data index can be used for prompt flows or the Copilot chat playground.

Step 2: Using a Prompt Flow with RAG

Create a Prompt Flow Project

Go to the AI Foundry portal and select **Prompt flow**. Click **New flow** and choose RAG (if available) or custom flow template, as highlighted in Figure 4-7.

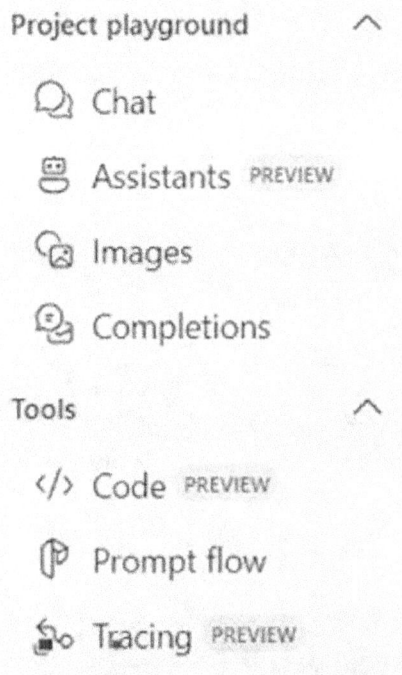

Figure 4-7. *Create prompt flow in AI Foundry*

As shown in Figure 4-8, scroll to the bottom of the page and click **Add your data**.

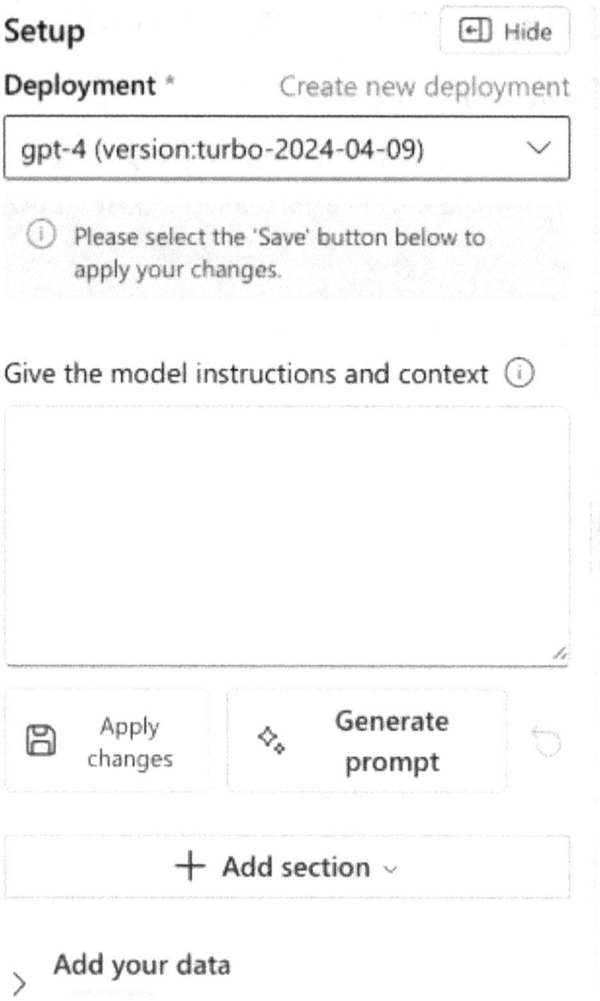

CHAPTER 4   BRINGING YOUR OWN DATA TO AI FOUNDRY

Figure 4-8. *Add data to prompt flow*

Select the data source from where the data resides, as shown in Figure 4-9.

CHAPTER 4   BRINGING YOUR OWN DATA TO AI FOUNDRY

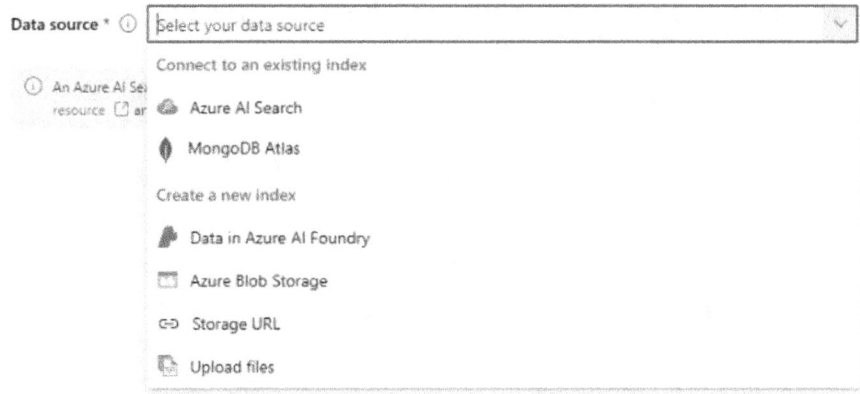

Figure 4-9. Select data source

After selecting the data source, click **Next** and **Choose index storage**. If you have Azure AI Search, browse and select from the drop-down menu, as shown in Figure 4-10.

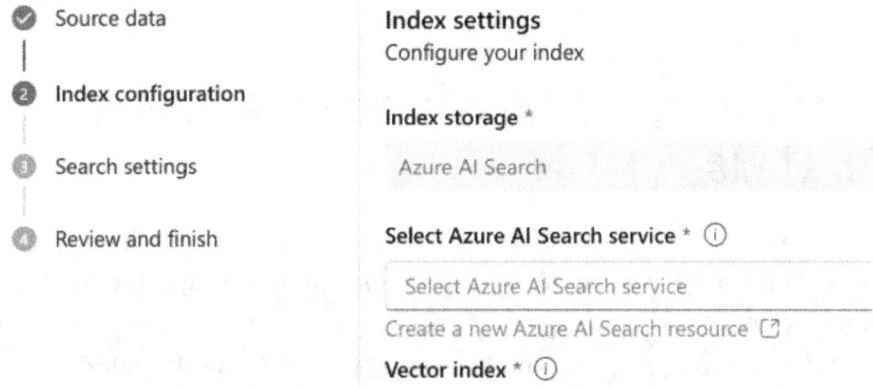

Figure 4-10. Select Azure AI Search

Once the index is created, you must use it in the prompt flow. In the Azure AI Foundry portal, select **Prompt flow**, and open an existing prompt flow or create a new one.

101

CHAPTER 4　BRINGING YOUR OWN DATA TO AI FOUNDRY

At the top of the menu, click **More tools** and choose **Index lookup**, and provide the name of the index lookup as shown in Figure 4-11.

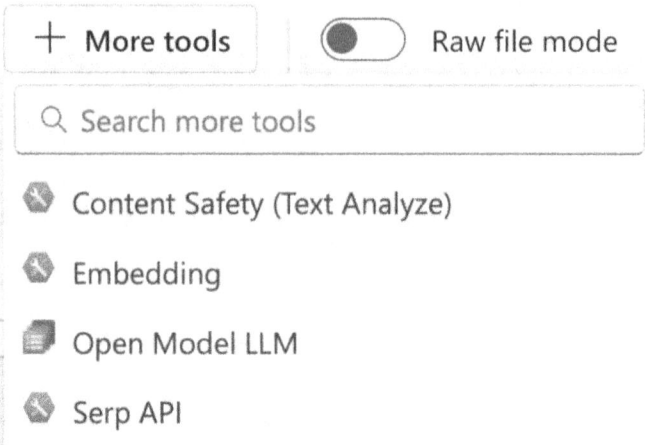

Figure 4-11. AI Foundry index lookup

Connecting and Managing Data Stores for LLMs

This section explores how to manage data sources in AI Foundry. Once data is added, it can be used as a source for indexing in the AI Foundry portal.

While creating the data, you have to set the data type. AI Foundry supports folder and file data types.

Folder means read files from the folder (see Figure 4-12).

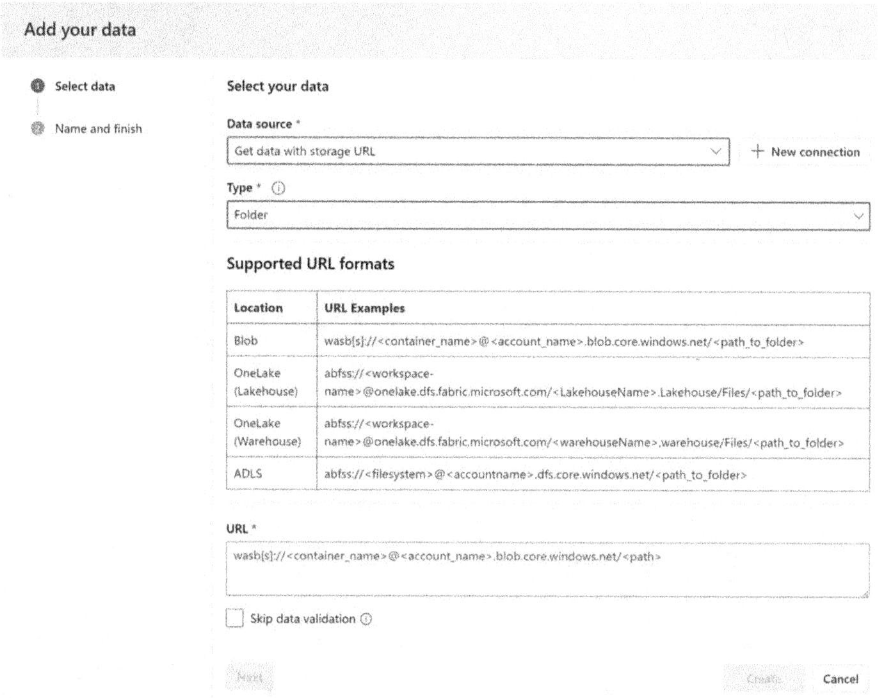

CHAPTER 4 BRINGING YOUR OWN DATA TO AI FOUNDRY

Figure 4-12. Create data from folder type in AI Foundry

File means read a single file from Azure Storage (see Figure 4-13).

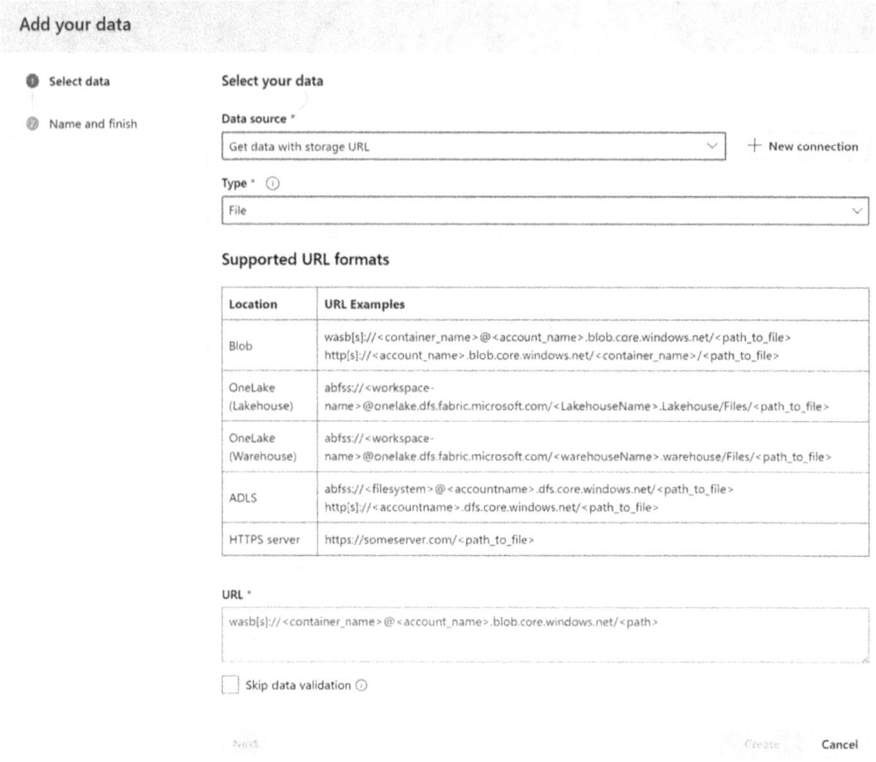

CHAPTER 4 BRINGING YOUR OWN DATA TO AI FOUNDRY

Figure 4-13. Select file type

Based on your file type selection, after entering the information, click **Next** and enter the name of the data source, as shown in Figure 4-14.

CHAPTER 4 BRINGING YOUR OWN DATA TO AI FOUNDRY

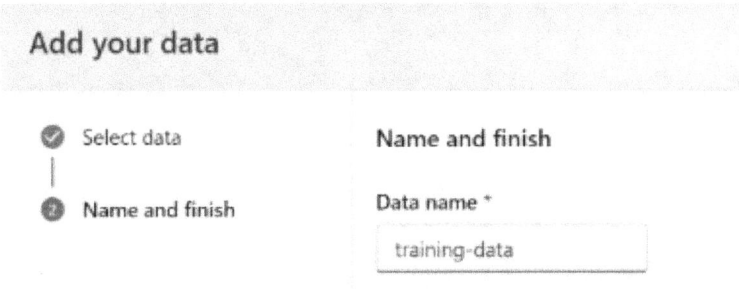

Figure 4-14. *Add data source name*

The data source has been created in AI Foundry.

Conclusion

This chapter explored one of the most impactful advancements in generative AI applications: retrieval-augmented generation. You began by learning about RAG and why it matters, especially when dealing with dynamic, domain-specific, or proprietary information that traditional LLMs cannot access by default. Finally, you learned how to connect and manage data stores, organize documents, and create indexes that make your enterprise knowledge accessible to AI models—all while maintaining control, security, and performance.

With RAG in place, your LLM applications are no longer confined to static knowledge—they can now reason over and respond based on your organization's own data assets.

Moving forward, you'll build on this capability to explore multimodal AI services, combining text, speech, vision, and documents to create even more interactive and intelligent applications. RAG lays the groundwork, and the next chapter shows how to bring richer context and inputs into your AI solutions.

CHAPTER 5

Exploring Multimodal AI Capabilities

The previous chapter explored how retrieval-augmented generation (RAG) enhances large language models (LLMs) by grounding their responses in enterprise-specific knowledge. You learned how to set up a RAG infrastructure, design prompt flows that leverage external knowledge, and manage connected data stores. Now, let's shift focus from text-driven intelligence to the expansive world of multimodal AI.

Modern AI is no longer limited to understanding and generating text. With advancements, AI systems can now perceive and interpret the world more like humans do—processing images, understanding spoken language, and extracting insights from complex documents.

This chapter covers the following topics.

- Azure AI Speech, Azure AI Vision, and Azure AI Document Intelligence
- Azure AI Vision's capabilities
- Using Azure AI Document Intelligence with prompt flow
- Protecting sensitive information with PII detection

CHAPTER 5 EXPLORING MULTIMODAL AI CAPABILITIES

AI Portfolio

The Azure Multimodal AI & LLM Processing Accelerator is a one-stop shop for all AI+LLM use cases like data extraction, enrichment, and classification. It supports a variety of input data, including text, documents, images, and audio.

Single-model AI/single modality AI has a single modality, which only works on one data type using a single AI model, as shown in Figure 5-1. Consider an example of chat-based GPT where you give input prompts in the form of text and generate output in text format.

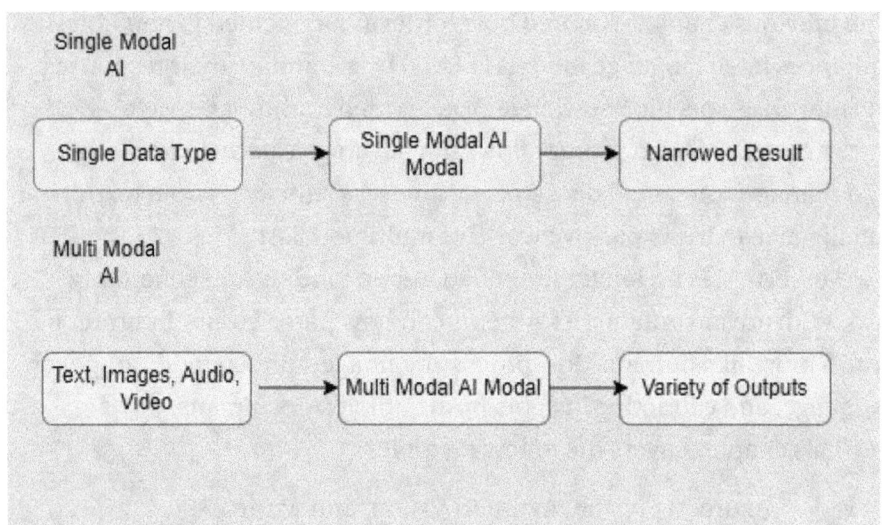

Figure 5-1. *Single modal and multimodal AI*

Multimodal AI can take input in the form of text, images, audio, videos, or charts, and the AI model can generate output.

Artificial intelligence has two main areas: predictive AI and generative AI. Predictive AI and generative AI are two branches of AI technologies that use machine learning and deep learning algorithms.

CHAPTER 5   EXPLORING MULTIMODAL AI CAPABILITIES

Figure 5-2 illustrates Microsoft's AI portfolio architecture. AI developers and data scientists can use Azure's cognitive services, including Azure AI Speech, Azure AI Vision, Azure AI Document Intelligence, and the Azure OpenAI. Let's also examine each of these services in detail. These cognitive services can be integrated with applications like Microsoft Power BI, Microsoft Power Apps, and Microsoft Dynamics 365 to leverage the AI capabilities.

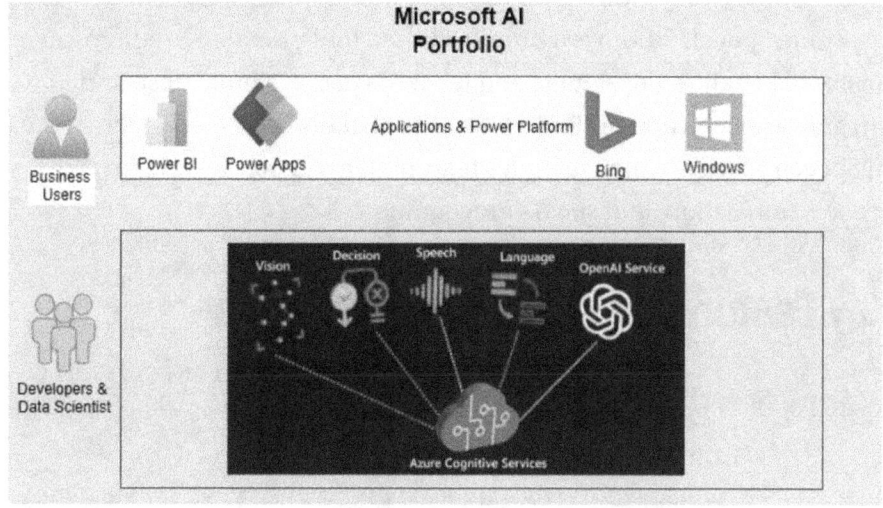

Figure 5-2. *Microsoft's AI portfolio*

Azure AI Speech provides speech-to-text and text-to-speech capabilities as highlighted in Figure 5-3. With the speech service, you can create custom voices and specific words based on the vocabulary or build your own models. Speech is available in many languages and regions.

Figure 5-3. Azure AI Speech services

Azure Speech Studio is a browser-based tool provided by Microsoft Azure that enables developers and business users to build, test, and integrate speech capabilities into their applications. It's part of the Azure AI Speech service, which includes features like speech-to-text, text-to-speech, translation, and speaker recognition.

Key Features of Azure Speech Studio

- **Speech to text (STT)**
  - Convert spoken audio into text.
  - Use real-time or batch transcription.
  - Customize models with domain-specific vocabulary using custom speech.

- **Text to speech (TTS)**
  - Convert text into lifelike speech using neural voices.
  - Choose from 400+ voices across 140+ languages.
  - Customize voice style, pitch, speed, and pronunciation using SSML (Speech Synthesis Markup Language).
  - Create your own neural voice using custom neural voice (with Microsoft approval).

- **Custom neural voice**

  – Design a unique branded voice for applications (e.g., virtual assistants, call centers).

  – Requires legal and ethical approval from Microsoft.

  – Record and upload voice data for training.

- **Speech translation**

  – Offers real-time translation from one spoken language to another.

  – Supports 70+ languages for recognition and 100+ for text translation.

- **Intent recognition and command and control**

  Integrate with LUIS or Azure Language Understanding to recognize intents from spoken language.

- **Speaker recognition**

  – Identify or verify speakers by voice.

  – Useful for authentication or voice-based personalization.

To use Azure Speech Studio, go to `https://speech.microsoft.com`. Now let's review the step-by-step process.

First, sign in with your Azure account. Select a speech service region and resource, as seen in Figure 5-4.

CHAPTER 5 EXPLORING MULTIMODAL AI CAPABILITIES

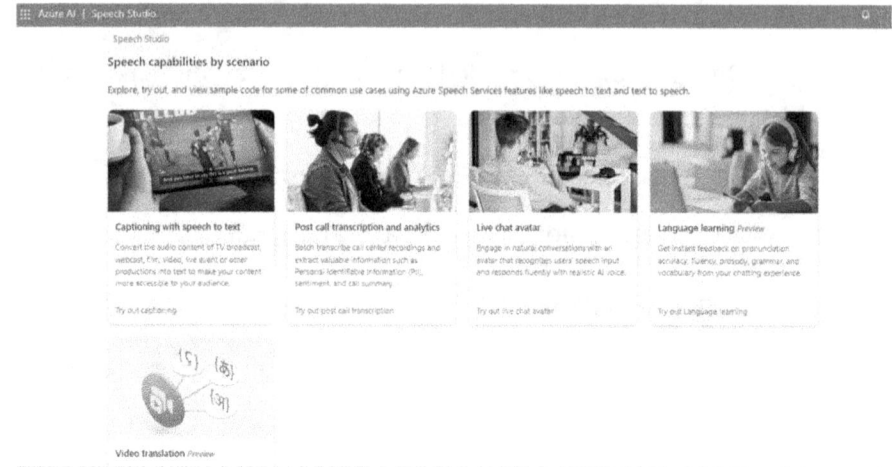

Figure 5-4. Azure AI Speech services

Next, choose the service you'd like to use. They are described as follows.

- **Speech-to-text**: With this feature, you can enable both batch and real-time transcription. As shown in Figure 5-5, you can click **Playgrounds** and select **Speech playground** to experiment with the speech service.

Figure 5-5. Speech playground

CHAPTER 5 EXPLORING MULTIMODAL AI CAPABILITIES

- It supports
  - Real-time transcription
  - Batch transcription
  - Fast transcription
  - Custom speech
- **Text to speech**: With the text-to-speech feature, you can enable your applications or tools to convert text into speech. It is also known as speech synthesis. Table 5-1 summarizes the core features of this feature.

Table 5-1. *Text-to-Speech Services*

Feature	Usage
Standard Voice	Natural voices
Custom Voice	Self-service to create a natural brand voice

- **Speech translation**: Real-time speech translation allows developers to convert language into text and translate it into multiple languages in real-time, making it ideal for building applications like multilingual virtual assistants, live translation tools, or subtitling systems. It has the following features.
  - Real-Time speed to text translation
  - Supports 100+ languages and variants
  - Speaker identification when multiple speakers are present
  - Text-to-speech output
  - Custom voice and translation models

Let's explore how you can run your application to translate speech from one language to text in another language. To set up an environment to use a Python script, download and install the Python SDK available on the PyPI module. You need to set the environment variables depending on your operating system. In Windows, it is similar to the following.

- *setx SPEECH_KEY your-key*
- *setx ENDPOINT your-endpoint*

Create a new Python file after installing the package using the following command.

```
pip install azure-cognitiveservices-speech
```

The following is sample code for a Python file.

```
import os
import azure.cognitiveservices.speech as speechsdk

def recognize_from_microphone():
    speech_translation_config = speechsdk.translation.Speech
TranslationConfig(subscription=os.environ.get('SPEECH_KEY'),
endpoint=os.environ.get('ENDPOINT'))
    speech_translation_config.speech_recognition_
language="en-US"

    to_language ="it"
    speech_translation_config.add_target_language(to_language)

    audio_config = speechsdk.audio.AudioConfig(use_default_
microphone=True)
    translation_recognizer = speechsdk.translation.TranslationR
ecognizer(translation_config=speech_translation_config, audio_
config=audio_config)

    print("Speak into your microphone.")
```

```
    translation_recognition_result = translation_recognizer.
recognize_once_async().get()

    if translation_recognition_result.reason == speechsdk.
ResultReason.TranslatedSpeech:
        print("Recognized: {}".format(translation_recognition_
result.text))
        print("""Translated into '{}': {}""".format(
            to_language,
            translation_recognition_result.translations[to_
language]))
    elif translation_recognition_result.reason == speechsdk.
ResultReason.NoMatch:
        print("No speech could be recognized: {}".
format(translation_recognition_result.no_match_details))
    elif translation_recognition_result.reason == speechsdk.
ResultReason.Canceled:
        cancellation_details = translation_recognition_result.
cancellation_details
        print("Speech Recognition canceled: {}".
format(cancellation_details.reason))
        if cancellation_details.reason == speechsdk.
CancellationReason.Error:
            print("Error details: {}".format(cancellation_
details.error_details))

recognize_from_microphone()
```

Now, from the application console, start the speech recognition from the microphone and speak into your microphone when prompted.

It is also possible to do video translation in Azure AI Speech. You can create immersive, localized video for various use cases as follows.

CHAPTER 5   EXPLORING MULTIMODAL AI CAPABILITIES

- News and media organizations
- Advertisements and marketing
- Education
- Files, TV shows, and vlogs

Go to Azure AI Foundry, select Azure AI Speech, and click the **Video translation** feature, as shown in Figure 5-6.

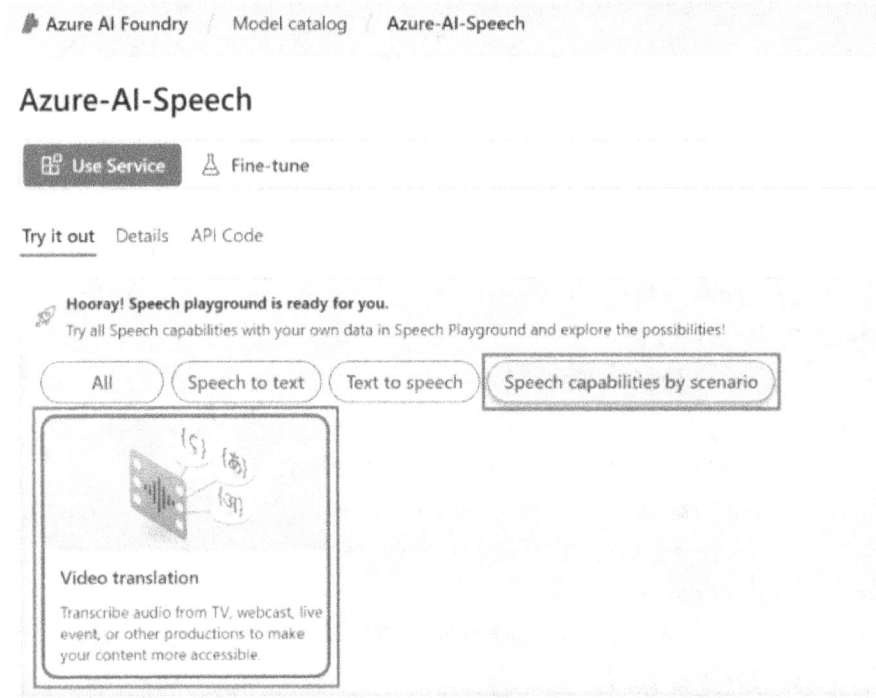

Figure 5-6. *AI Foundry video translation*

CHAPTER 5   EXPLORING MULTIMODAL AI CAPABILITIES

- **Voice Live API**: This feature is used for low-latency, high-quality speech-to-speech interaction for voice agents. It helps AI developers to scale and manage voice-driven experiences to reduce the manual efforts to orchestrate multiple components. This feature can be used in various scenarios.
  - Interactive bots for customer support
  - Automotive voice assistants for car navigation
  - Government and public services to assist people with administrative questions

---

Note   At the time of writing this book, this feature was a public preview feature.

You can test features interactively with audio samples or real-time input.

Finally, download audio, transcripts, or SSML to integrate into your applications.

Azure AI Vision's Capabilities

The Azure AI Vision Image Analysis and Azure AI Face services feature capabilities such as analyzing images and detecting objects or human faces. Table 5-2 provides more information. To experiment with these capabilities, go to https://portal.vision.cognitive.azure.com/ and sign in. Once you are signed in, the screen shown in Figure 5-7 appears.

CHAPTER 5　EXPLORING MULTIMODAL AI CAPABILITIES

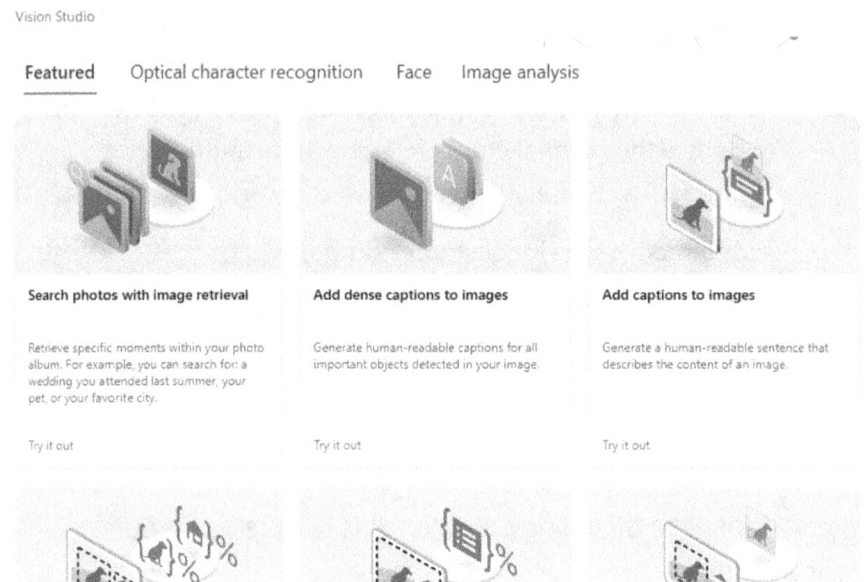

Figure 5-7. *Azure AI Vision services*

Table 5-2. *Azure AI Vision types*

Vision Type	Description
Image analysis	Detect, classify, and generate insights
Spatial analysis	Learn people's movements in real time
Facial recognition	Verify human identity
OCR	Extract text from images

Azure Image Analysis has the ability to read text, analyze images, and detect faces with technologies like machine learning and optical character recognition (OCR). Computer vision is a core AI area that enables applications to see the world by processing images.

The Azure AI Face service consists of algorithms to detect, recognize, and analyze human faces from images. It is useful in various scenarios, such as validating user identity based on the trusted image, and liveness detection to check whether a person is physically present.

CHAPTER 5 EXPLORING MULTIMODAL AI CAPABILITIES

Now let's build a prompt flow for image analysis with Azure AI Foundry.

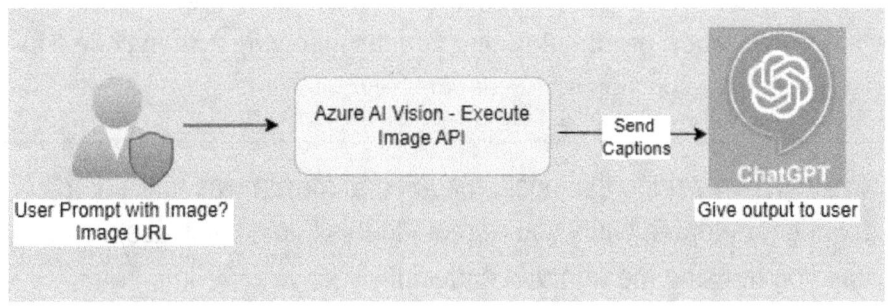

Figure 5-8. *Prompt flow architecture with Azure AI Vision*

As Figure 5-8 illustrates, a user has a query about a specific image for which they want more information. The user provides the image URL as input. This URL is given to the input, which makes an API call that extracts information from the image and generates human-readable captions that can be fed to the LLM model to generate output to the user.

From the Azure portal, sign in and click **Compute vision** to create a compute vision instance. Once the compute vision instance is deployed, you can click **Vision Studio** to explore all features of Azure AI compute vision as highlighted in Figure 5-9.

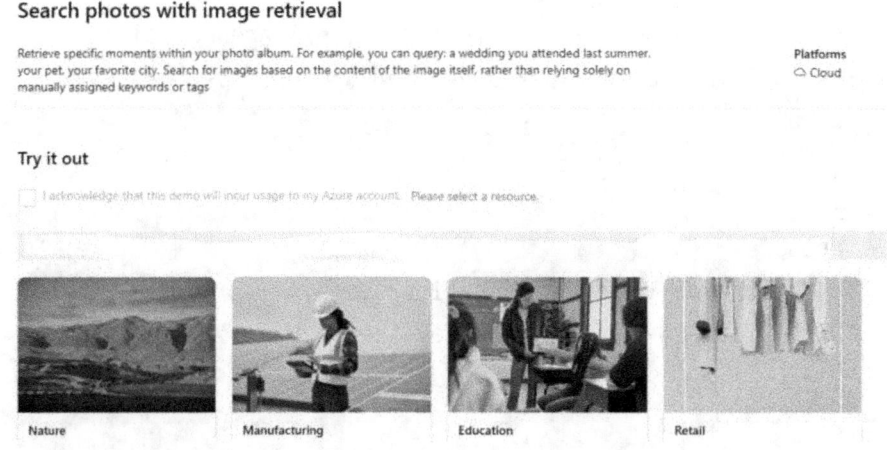

Figure 5-9. *AI Vision photo search and image retrieval*

CHAPTER 5 EXPLORING MULTIMODAL AI CAPABILITIES

Here you can upload a photo or use an existing image to find more information about the specific image. Now, from the Azure AI Foundry portal, create a new prompt flow and add the following Python code. This is supported in a specific pricing tier and region.

Note When writing this book, the API end format was utilized; it might get outdated while you're reading this book, so please make sure you're using the right API endpoint.

---

image_analysis:

```
import os
import json
import requests
from promptflow import tool

key="YOUR_PRIMARY_KEY"
endpoint = "YOUR_CV_ENDPOINT"

@tool
def analyse_image(image_url: str) -> str:
    url = str(endpoint) + "computervision/imageanalysis:analyze?api-version=2024-02-01&features=denseCaptions"
    data = {
        "url": image_url
    }
    headers = {
        "Content-Type":"application/json",
        "Ocp-Apim-Subscription-Key":key
    }
```

```
result = requests.post(url = url, headers = headers,
json=data).json()

dense_captions=""

if (result['denseCaptionsResult']):
    for caption in result['denseCaptionsResult']['values']:
        dense_captions = dense_captions +
        caption["text"] + "\n"

return dense_captions
```

Summarisation

```
# system:
You will be provided with multiple captions for an image that
is analysed using azure computer vision resource.
Your work is to answer the user query based upon information
grabbed about the image from these dense captions.

If you do not have sufficient knowledge about the image from
these dense captions to answer the user query
then please respond with:
"I am sorry but I don't have sufficient knowledge to answer
your query"

# user:
user query: {{question}}
dense captions: {{dense_captions}}
```

Once it is ready, you have to set up the connection, add the deployment name, and enter the prompt to receive the response of the prompt flow.

CHAPTER 5   EXPLORING MULTIMODAL AI CAPABILITIES

Using Azure AI Document Intelligence with Prompt Flows

Azure AI Document Intelligence is a cloud service that automatically uses AI and machine learning to read, analyze, and extract key information from documents like PDFs, scanned forms, invoices, receipts, and ID cards. It is a cloud-based AI service from Microsoft that enables organizations to extract structured data from unstructured documents such as invoices, receipts, contracts, and forms. Leveraging advanced machine learning models and OCR, it can identify key-value pairs, tables, and handwritten text, allowing businesses to automate data entry, improve accuracy, and accelerate document processing workflows. With capabilities to use prebuilt models or train custom models tailored to specific document types, Azure AI Document Intelligence seamlessly integrates into enterprise applications and scales efficiently across various industries.

Let's say you want to extract data like invoice number, date, and total amount from a set of invoice PDFs, and then summarize it using Azure OpenAI inside a prompt flow.

Step 1: Set up Azure AI Document Intelligence

Go to the Azure portal. Create a resource: Azure AI Document Intelligence as seen in Figure 5-10.

- Subscription
- Resource Group
- Region
- Name
- Pricing tier

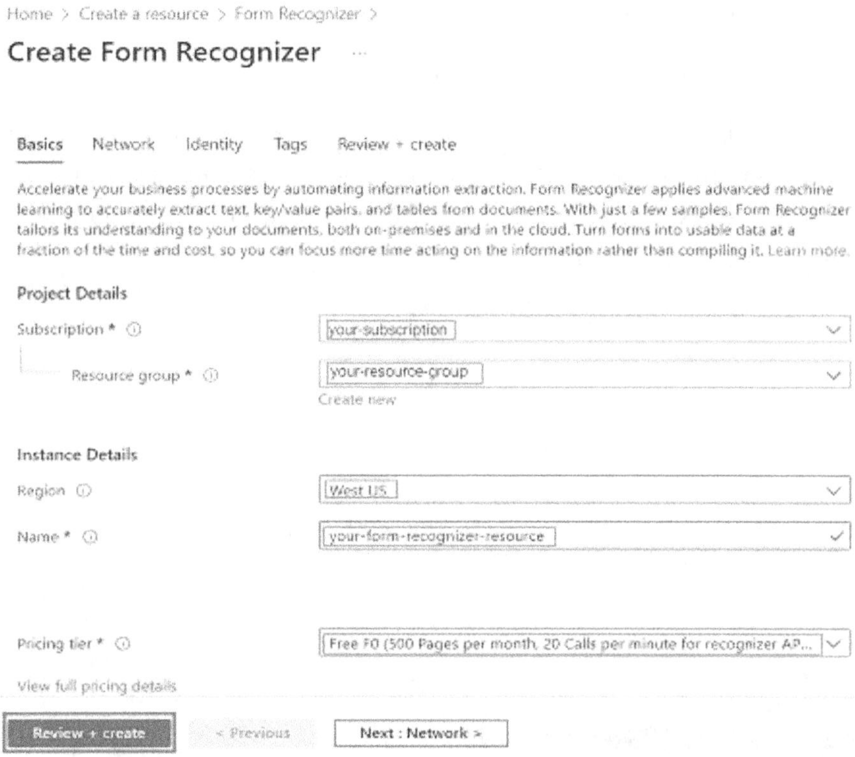

CHAPTER 5   EXPLORING MULTIMODAL AI CAPABILITIES

Figure 5-10. *Azure AI Foundry Document Intelligence*

Once the details are entered, the Document Intelligence resource is created. Take note of the URL and endpoint. Document intelligence can be used from the Document Intelligence portal or the AI Foundry Portal. You can build prebuilt and custom models with Azure AI Document Intelligence.

Step 2: Upload Sample Invoices

To upload data to be used in the Azure AI Document Intelligence, you must set up an Azure Blob Storage account. You need to have an Azure storage account to create a container. The following role assignments should be on your storage account to upload and use data for Azure AI Document Intelligence.

CHAPTER 5   EXPLORING MULTIMODAL AI CAPABILITIES

- Cognitive services user
- Storage blob data contributor

Cross-origin resource sharing (CORS) should also be enabled on your storage account to be accessible from the Document Intelligence Studio. Go to the Azure storage account from the portal and configure CORS as highlighted in Figure 5-11.

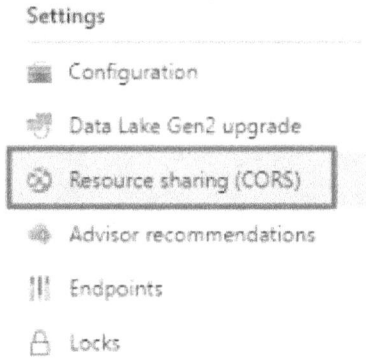

Figure 5-11. CORS configuration

Now create a new CORS entry for your blob storage. Set the allowed origins to `https://documentintelligence.ai.azure.com` as shown in Figure 5-12.

Figure 5-12. Allowed origins for blob storage

Sign in to the Azure portal, go to your blob storage, and upload files in the container as shown in Figure 5-13.

CHAPTER 5   EXPLORING MULTIMODAL AI CAPABILITIES

Figure 5-13. Upload files to blob storage

Step 3: Test Document Intelligence in AI Foundry

Open Azure AI Foundry. Select Document Intelligence Studio. Use the prebuilt invoice model.

Upload a sample invoice. Review extracted fields like the following.

- Vendor Name
- Invoice ID
- Due Date
- Amount Due

Once the document is uploaded and linked to Document Intelligence Studio, it auto-labels documents with prebuilt models. In the case of duplicates, duplicate labels are also detected, as shown in Figure 5-14.

125

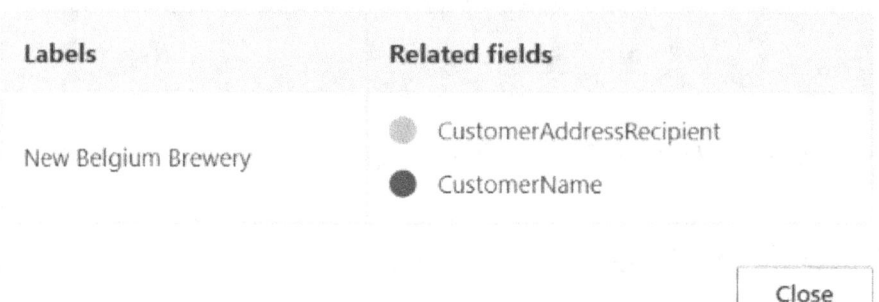

Figure 5-14. Document Intelligence Studio: duplicated labels

Step 4: Create a Prompt Flow

In Azure AI Foundry, go to **Prompt flow**. Create a new prompt flow project (e.g., Invoice Flow).

Define the following components.

- Document loader: Reads PDF invoice.

- Document Intelligence node: Extracts fields using Azure AI Document Intelligence.

- LLM prompt node: Sends extracted data to Azure OpenAI to generate a summary.

- Output node: Saves the final summary.

Microsoft Power Automate makes it possible to create a workflow using Azure Logic Apps and Azure AI Document Intelligence.

Let's go over the process of creating a workflow using Microsoft Power Automate.

CHAPTER 5   EXPLORING MULTIMODAL AI CAPABILITIES

Go to Power Automate, click **My flows** from the left pane, and then select **New flow ▶ Instant cloud flow** as highlighted in Figure 5-15.

Name your flow, select **Manually trigger a flow**, and then select **Create**.

You can also add input and upload files.

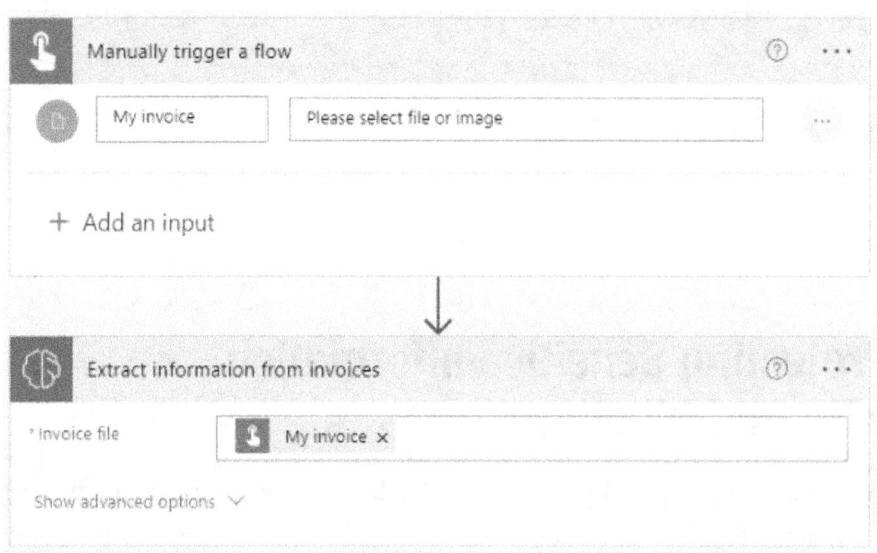

Figure 5-15. *Logic apps workflow*

Step 5: Design a Prompt

Let's look at an example prompt for the LLM.

You are an invoice analyst. Based on the following extracted invoice data, generate a summary.

Invoice Number: {{invoice_number}}
Vendor: {{vendor_name}}
Total Amount: {{amount_total}}
Due Date: {{due_date}}

Summary:

127

Step 6: Run the Flow

Run the prompt flow with multiple invoice PDFs.
　The result provides structured summaries, like the following.

> "Invoice 12345 from ABC Ltd. has a total amount of $4200, due by June 30, 2025."

Step 7: Deployment

Deploy your prompt flow as an endpoint. Trigger it via Logic App, Power Automate, or REST API when a new document arrives.

Protecting Sensitive Information with PII Detection

Personally Identifiable Information (PII) detection is a feature of Azure AI Language, specifically under the Text Analytics API, that helps identify and redact sensitive data such as the following.

- Names
- Addresses
- Email addresses
- Phone numbers
- Credit card numbers
- Government IDs (like SSNs, Aadhaar)
- Health-related information

This is critical for ensuring privacy compliance (e.g., GDPR, HIPAA) and responsible AI in applications that process user data. Azure AI Language is a cloud-based service with a natural language processing (NLP) feature to learn and analyze text. PII detection uses machine learning models trained on large datasets to scan and extract PII entities from unstructured text. The output includes the following.

- Entity type (e.g., phoneNumber, email, person, etc.)
- Confidence score
- Offset (position in the original text)

The following is an example.

```
{
  "text": "My name is John Doe and my email is john@example.com.",
  "piiEntities": [
    { "text": "John Doe", "category": "Person", "confidenceScore": 0.99 },
    { "text": "john@example.com", "category": "Email", "confidenceScore": 0.98         }
  ]
}
```

Azure AI Language PII detection uses Named Entity Recognition to identify and redact the sensitive information from the input data. It classifies sensitive personal data into predefined categories. It currently supports the following capabilities.

- Text PII: It is used to detect PII information from the text. Go to the Azure AI Foundry portal, click Playgrounds in the left pane, and then Try the Language playground, as shown in Figure 5-16.

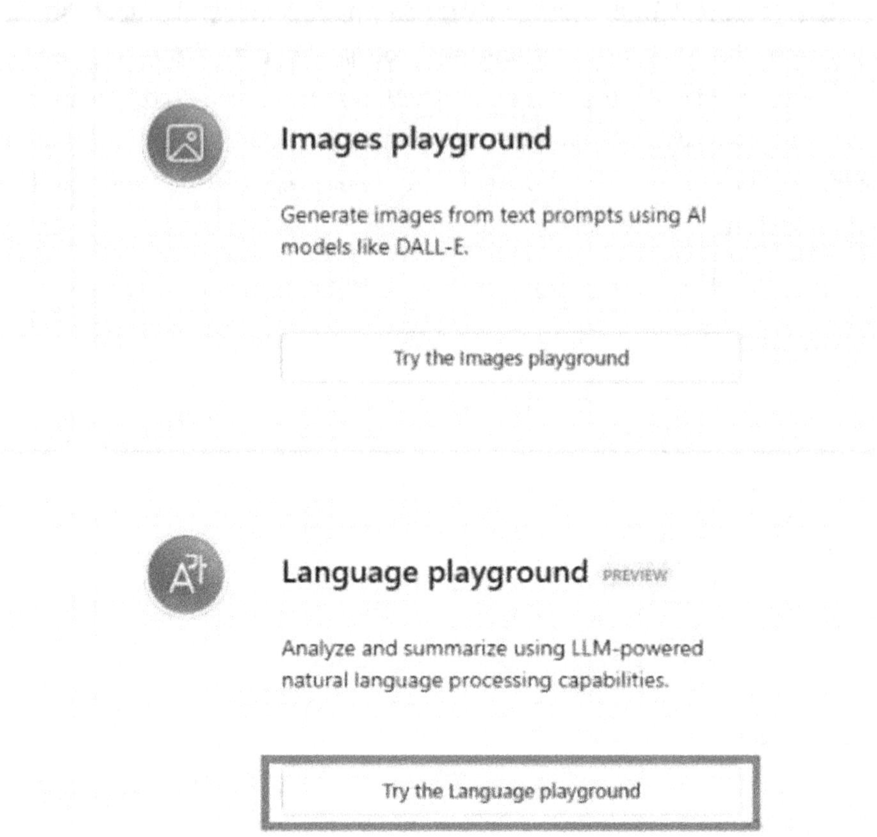

CHAPTER 5　EXPLORING MULTIMODAL AI CAPABILITIES

Images playground

Generate images from text prompts using AI models like DALL-E.

Try the Images playground

Language playground PREVIEW

Analyze and summarize using LLM-powered natural language processing capabilities.

Try the Language playground

Figure 5-16. *Language playground in AI Foundry*

- To extract PII information, you must configure the following, as highlighted in Figure 5-17.

    – API version

    – Model version

    – Text language

CHAPTER 5   EXPLORING MULTIMODAL AI CAPABILITIES

- Types to include
- Redaction policy
- Redaction character

Figure 5-17. *Language playground configurations*

- **Conversation PII**: It is a specialized model created to process audio conversations to detect and remove PII-sensitive information.

- **Native Document PII**: Using the HTTP POST request, you can transmit your data or document, and use the HTTP GET request to check the status of the request.

Conclusion

This chapter explored the powerful multimodal capabilities of Azure AI Studio that go beyond text—extending into speech, vision, and document intelligence. You saw how AI can extract insights from images, understand spoken language, and analyze documents at scale—making it easier for enterprises to automate and enhance content comprehension.

CHAPTER 5   EXPLORING MULTIMODAL AI CAPABILITIES

You also explored the chat playground with vision capabilities, where models can interpret and respond to visual prompts. This feature opens new possibilities for building intelligent assistants that can see and reason—ideal for industries like retail, healthcare, and manufacturing.

Additionally, you learned how to integrate Azure AI Document Intelligence with a prompt flow—enabling seamless document parsing, summarization, and transformation pipelines, all within a low-code environment. Finally, the chapter discussed protecting sensitive data using PII detection, ensuring your AI solutions remain safe, compliant, and trustworthy.

These foundational capabilities empower you to build multimodal AI workflows that are intelligent and responsible.

CHAPTER 6

Deploying, Monitoring, and Ensuring AI Safety

As you journey from ideation to implementation in generative AI, the ability to operationalize AI models becomes paramount. Building a compelling prompt flow is just the beginning—real value is realized when these solutions are deployed, monitored, and seamlessly integrated into enterprise applications and experiences.

This chapter explores the crucial transition from development to deployment. You'll learn how to deploy and debug prompt flows, ensuring your workflows are functional and optimized for performance and safety. You'll guide you through the process of consuming Azure AI Foundry endpoints—turning powerful AI workflows into reusable, scalable services.

Whether you're a data scientist, solution architect, or product leader, this chapter equips you with the tools and information to bring your AI solutions to life—securely, reliably, and at scale.

CHAPTER 6   DEPLOYING, MONITORING, AND ENSURING AI SAFETY

This chapter covers the following topics.

- Deploying and debugging prompt flows
- Consuming AI Foundry endpoints in applications
- Integrating AI Foundry with Copilot
- Monitoring and managing AI endpoints
- Security, governance, and AI trustworthiness

Deploying and Debugging Prompt Flows

Deployment is a process of taking whatever you build using the AI Foundry and creating endpoints that other outside AI Foundry projects can use. The AI Foundry model has a catalog of various models, which should be deployed so that users or projects can use them. AI Foundry has multiple deployment options for models, depending on the needs and requirements, as highlighted in Figure 6-1 and summarized in Table 6-1.

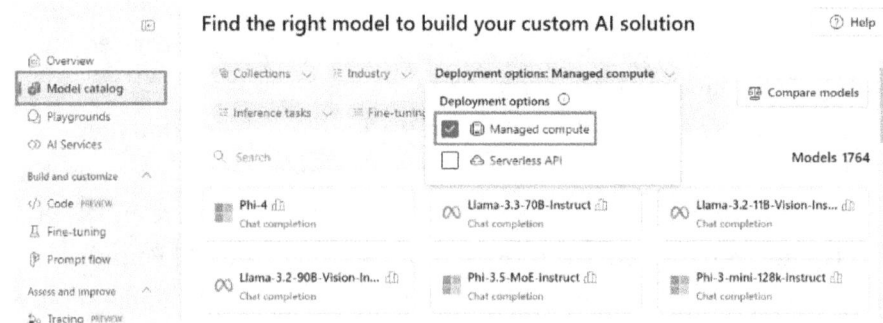

Figure 6-1. *AI Foundry deployment options*

- **AI Foundry models**: You can deploy models that are available in the AI Foundry model catalog.

134

CHAPTER 6   DEPLOYING, MONITORING, AND ENSURING AI SAFETY

- **Serverless API deployment**: In the serverless API deployment, the price is calculated per token. It doesn't require a compute quota from the Azure subscription.

- **Azure OpenAI**: It has a diverse set of models with different capabilities and price points. Model availability varies by region and cloud.

- **Open and custom models**: For custom and open models, you can host open models in your Azure subscription with a managed infrastructure and virtual machines.

Table 6-1. AI Foundry Deployment Options

	Azure OpenAI	AI Foundry Models	Serverless API Deployment	Open And Custom Models
Deployment Resource	Azure OpenAI Resource	Azure AI service resources	AI Project Resource	AI Project Resource
Requires Hub/Projects	No	No	Yes	Yes
Private Networking	Yes	Yes	Yes	Yes
Custom Content Filtering	Yes	Yes	No	No

(*continued*)

Table 6-1. (*continued*)

	Azure OpenAI	**AI Foundry Models**	**Serverless API Deployment**	**Open And Custom Models**
Use Case	OpenAI Models	To use flagship models in the Azure AI catalog	To use a single model from a specific provider	Use the OpenAI model and have enough compute quota in your subscription
Pricing	Token Usage and through units	Token Usage	Token Usage	Compute Core Hours
Keyless Authentication	Yes	Yes	Yes (if you configure the open and custom models properly, they also support keyless auth)	No

In the previous chapter, you learned how to create a prompt flow in the AI Foundry portal. Now, discuss how you can debug a prompt flow before moving to a production environment. To validate the prompt flow, you need to submit a batch run and use the evaluation method in the prompt flow. With a batch run, you can execute your prompt flow against the large dataset and generate the output. You can select various evaluation methods to compare the output of your prompt flow against your goal or acceptance criteria. Evaluation method is a special type of flow that calculates metrics for your prompt flow based on various aspects.

CHAPTER 6 DEPLOYING, MONITORING, AND ENSURING AI SAFETY

As you can see in Figure 6-2, from the AI Foundry portal, click the **Evaluate** option and select either **Custom evaluation** or **Built-in evaluation**. With custom evaluation, you can submit batch runs with or without the evaluation methods of your flow.

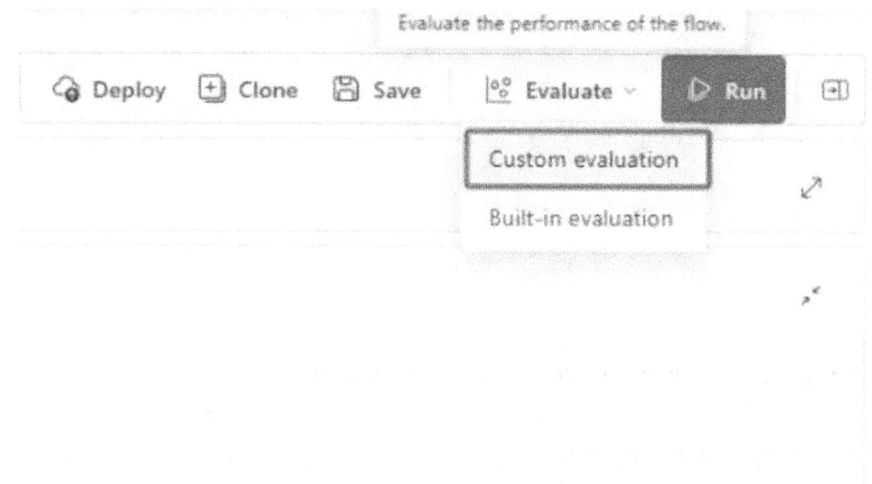

Figure 6-2. *AI Foundry custom and built-in evaluations*

You must first provide your batch run's display name and description, as shown in Figure 6-3.

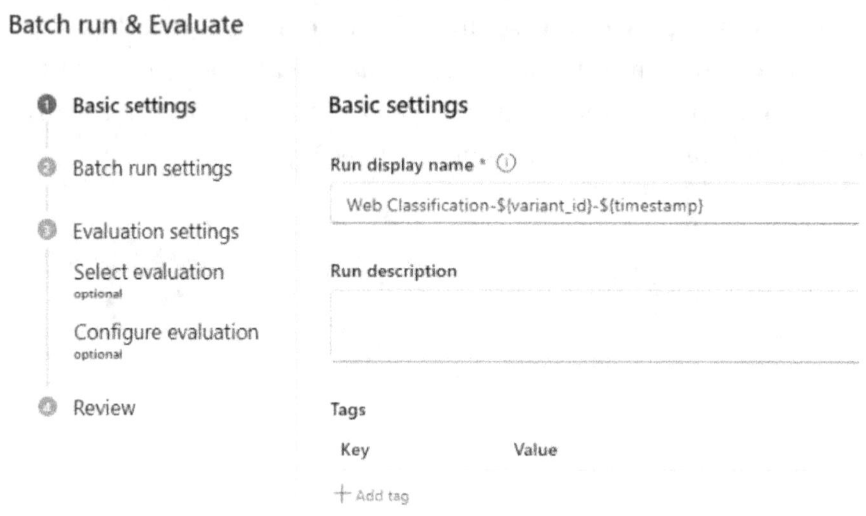

CHAPTER 6 DEPLOYING, MONITORING, AND ENSURING AI SAFETY

Batch run & Evaluate

① Basic settings

② Batch run settings

③ Evaluation settings
   Select evaluation
   optional
   Configure evaluation
   optional

④ Review

Basic settings

Run display name *
Web Classification-${variant_id}-${timestamp}

Run description

Tags
Key   Value
+ Add tag

Figure 6-3. *AI Foundry batch run evaluation*

The next step is to upload a dataset on which you want to test your flow by selecting available compute sessions. It also shows input mapping of your uploaded dataset and sample data preview as highlighted in Figure 6-4.

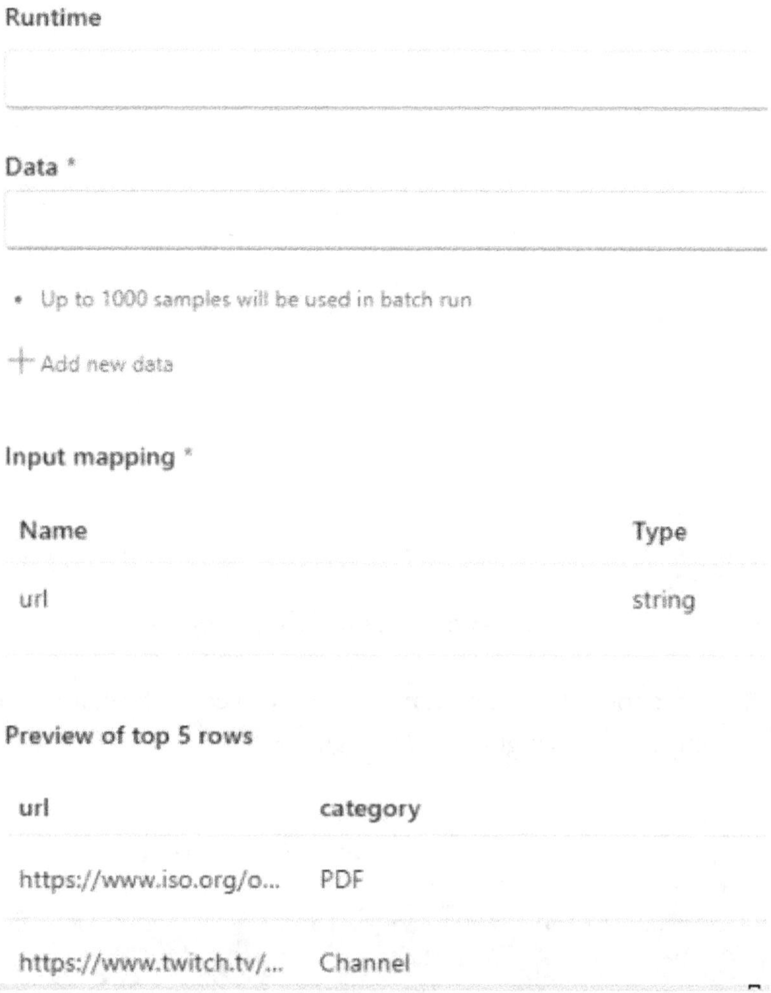

Runtime

Data *

- Up to 1000 samples will be used in batch run
- + Add new data

Input mapping *

Name	Type
url	string

Preview of top 5 rows

url	category
https://www.iso.org/o...	PDF
https://www.twitch.tv/...	Channel

Figure 6-4. *Upload dataset: mapping and data preview*

The next step is to choose the evaluation method to validate the performance of the flow, as highlighted in Figure 6-5.

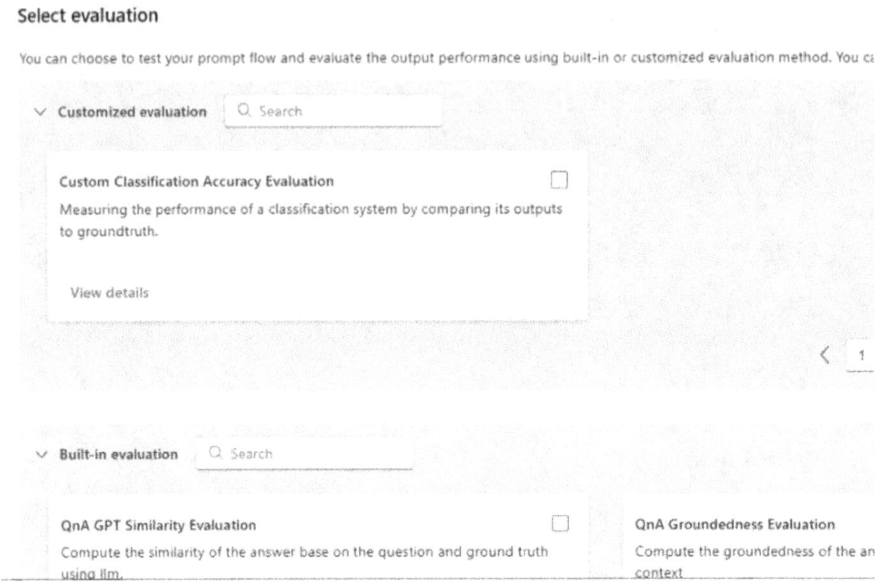

CHAPTER 6   DEPLOYING, MONITORING, AND ENSURING AI SAFETY

Select evaluation

You can choose to test your prompt flow and evaluate the output performance using built-in or customized evaluation method. You ca

∨ Customized evaluation   🔍 Search

  Custom Classification Accuracy Evaluation   ☐
  Measuring the performance of a classification system by comparing its outputs to groundtruth.

  View details

                                                                                          ⟨ 1

∨ Built-in evaluation   🔍 Search

  QnA GPT Similarity Evaluation   ☐   QnA Groundedness Evaluation
  Compute the similarity of the answer base on the question and ground truth using llm.   Compute the groundedness of the an context

Figure 6-5. *Choose evaluation method for prompt flow*

After you choose the evaluation method, you can submit the batch run and view the output as highlighted in Figure 6-6.

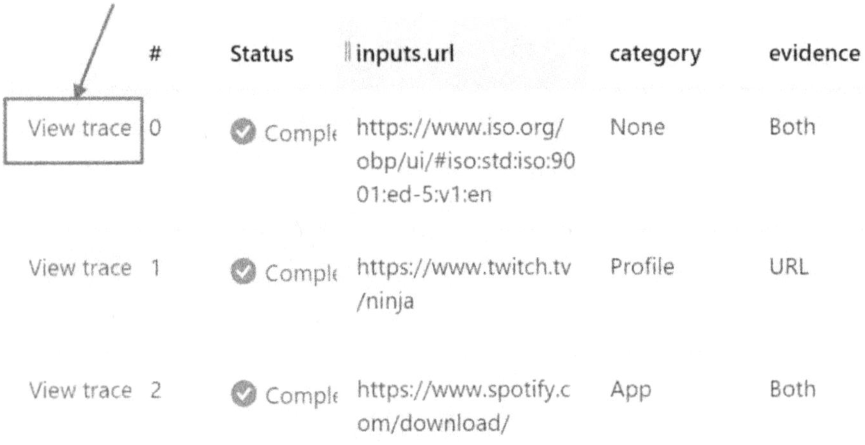

	#	Status	inputs.url	category	evidence
View trace	0	✅ Comple	https://www.iso.org/obp/ui/#iso:std:iso:9001:ed-5:v1:en	None	Both
View trace	1	✅ Comple	https://www.twitch.tv/ninja	Profile	URL
View trace	2	✅ Comple	https://www.spotify.com/download/	App	Both

Figure 6-6. *Prompt flow evaluation results*

CHAPTER 6 DEPLOYING, MONITORING, AND ENSURING AI SAFETY

Once the prompt flow output is ready, you can still select evaluation runs, and multiple evaluation outputs can be appended for comparison.

Let's go through the step-by-step model deployment process with a managed compute deployment option.

First, go to the AI Foundry portal and select the model catalog from the left pane as shown in Figure 6-7.

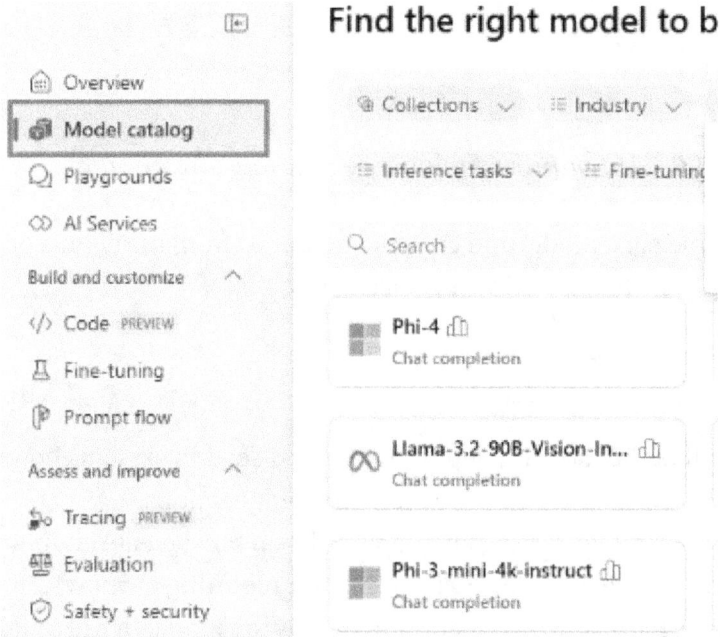

Figure 6-7. *AI Foundry model catalog*

Click **Deployment options** and select **Managed compute**, as shown in Figure 6-8.

141

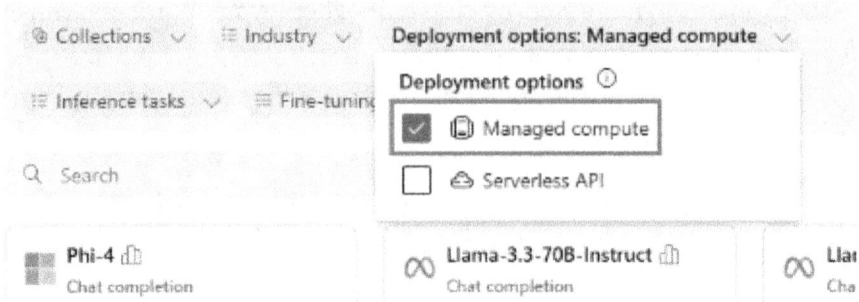

Figure 6-8. AI Foundry deployment: managed compute

Next, select a model and copy the model ID from the details page. Finally, install the following packages.

```
pip install azure-ai-ml
pip install azure-identity
```

Now that the model is deployed, the next section explains how to create endpoints and consume them in AI applications.

Once the model is built and deployed, you must create endpoints so others can use it in the application or for reporting purposes. In the previous section, you learned how to deploy the model in AI Foundry with options as managed computing.

The first step is to authenticate with Azure Machine Learning and create a client object.

```
from azure.ai.ml import MLClient
from azure.identity import InteractiveBrowserCredential

workspace_ml_client = MLClient(
    credential=InteractiveBrowserCredential(),
```

CHAPTER 6   DEPLOYING, MONITORING, AND ENSURING AI SAFETY

```
    subscription_id="your subscription name goes here",
    resource_group_name="your resource group name goes here",
    workspace_name="your project name goes here",
)
```

Use your subscription ID, resource group name, and workspace name in the preceding code snippet.

Now, for a managed compute option, the endpoint must be created before you can deploy it. An endpoint is similar to the container, where you can make multiple model deployments. Within a region, the endpoint name should be unique.

```
import time, sys
from azure.ai.ml.entities import (
    ManagedOnlineEndpoint,
    ManagedOnlineDeployment,
    ProbeSettings,
)

# Make the endpoint name unique
timestamp = int(time.time())
online_endpoint_name = "your endpoint name here" + str(timestamp)

# Create an online endpoint
endpoint = ManagedOnlineEndpoint(
    name=online_endpoint_name,
    auth_mode="key",
)
workspace_ml_client.online_endpoints.begin_create_or_update(endpoint).wait()
```

Once the endpoints are created, create a deployment using the model ID you got from the deployment in AI Foundry.

CHAPTER 6   DEPLOYING, MONITORING, AND ENSURING AI SAFETY

```
model_name = "azureml://registries/azureml/models/deepset-
roberta-base-squad2/versions/16"

demo_deployment = ManagedOnlineDeployment(
    name="demo",
    endpoint_name=online_endpoint_name,
    model=model_name,
    instance_type="Standard_DS3_v2",
    instance_count=2,
    liveness_probe=ProbeSettings(
        failure_threshold=30,
        success_threshold=1,
        timeout=2,
        period=10,
        initial_delay=100,
    ),
    readiness_probe=ProbeSettings(
        failure_threshold=10,
        success_threshold=1,
        timeout=10,
        period=10,
        initial_delay=1000,
    ),
)
Try:
workspace_ml_client.online_deployments.begin_create_or_
update(demo_deployment).wait()
endpoint.traffic = {"demo": 100}
workspace_ml_client.online_endpoints.begin_create_or_
update(endpoint).result()
Except:
   Print("Error....")
```

CHAPTER 6 DEPLOYING, MONITORING, AND ENSURING AI SAFETY

Once the model is deployed and the endpoint is created, it is ready to use. It can be used for actual production data to use for your application.

Integrating AI Foundry with Copilot

Microsoft Copilot is an AI-powered digital assistant designed to enhance productivity and creativity across various Microsoft platforms. It acts as a conversational chatbot, providing information, generating text and images, and automating tasks. Copilot integrates with Microsoft 365 apps like Word, Excel, and PowerPoint, as well as Windows and other services, to offer personalized support and streamline workflows.

So, copilots are very powerful, and you can make them more powerful by integrating prompt flow within AI Foundry. The Copilot Studio page is highlighted in Figure 6-9.

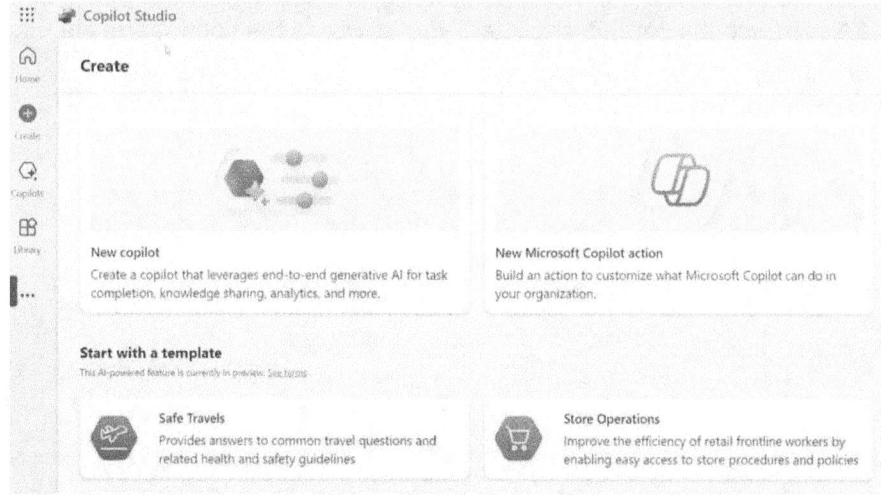

Figure 6-9. *Copilot Studio*

As shown in Figure 6-10, click **Create** to create a new copilot.

CHAPTER 6   DEPLOYING, MONITORING, AND ENSURING AI SAFETY

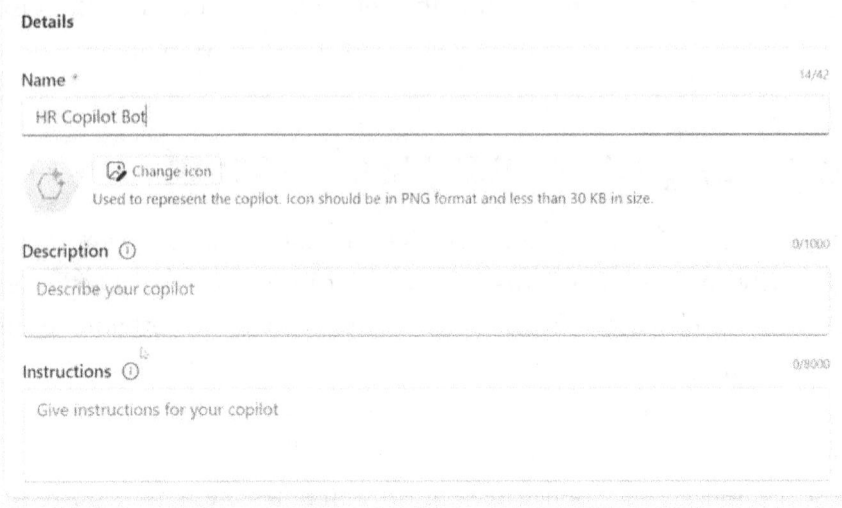

Figure 6-10. *Create a copilot*

Now, once the copilot is created, you can go to the copilot and click **Add action**, as shown in Figure 6-11.

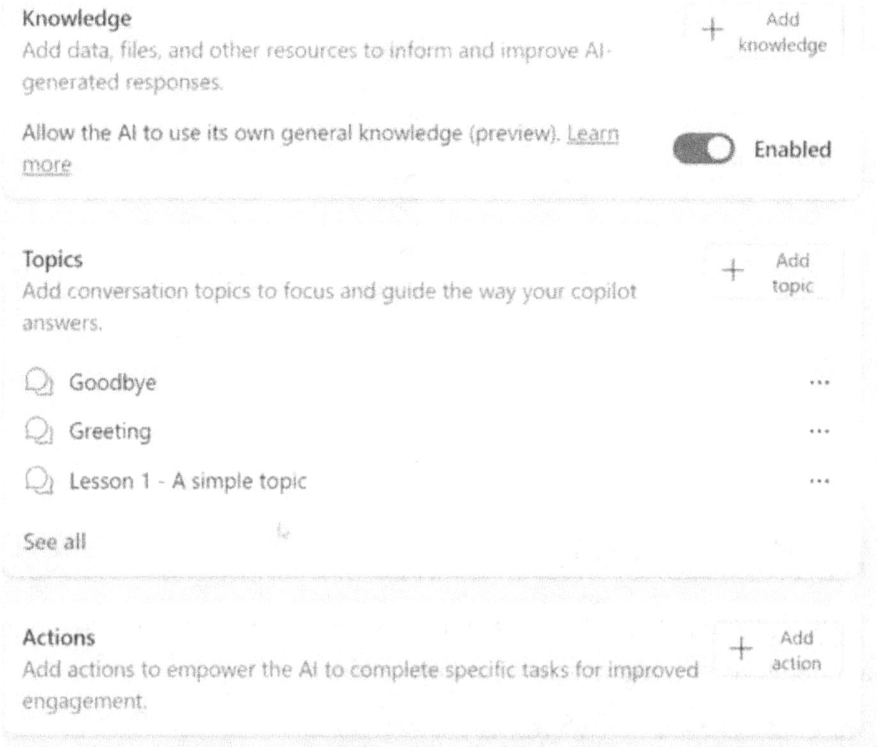

CHAPTER 6   DEPLOYING, MONITORING, AND ENSURING AI SAFETY

Knowledge
Add data, files, and other resources to inform and improve AI-generated responses.

+ Add knowledge

Allow the AI to use its own general knowledge (preview). Learn more

🔘 Enabled

Topics
Add conversation topics to focus and guide the way your copilot answers.

+ Add topic

💬 Goodbye   ...

💬 Greeting   ...

💬 Lesson 1 - A simple topic   ...

See all

Actions
Add actions to empower the AI to complete specific tasks for improved engagement.

+ Add action

***Figure 6-11.** Add actions in copilot*

Click **Flows** and select **Create a new flow** or use an existing prompt flow (see Figure 6-12).

CHAPTER 6 DEPLOYING, MONITORING, AND ENSURING AI SAFETY

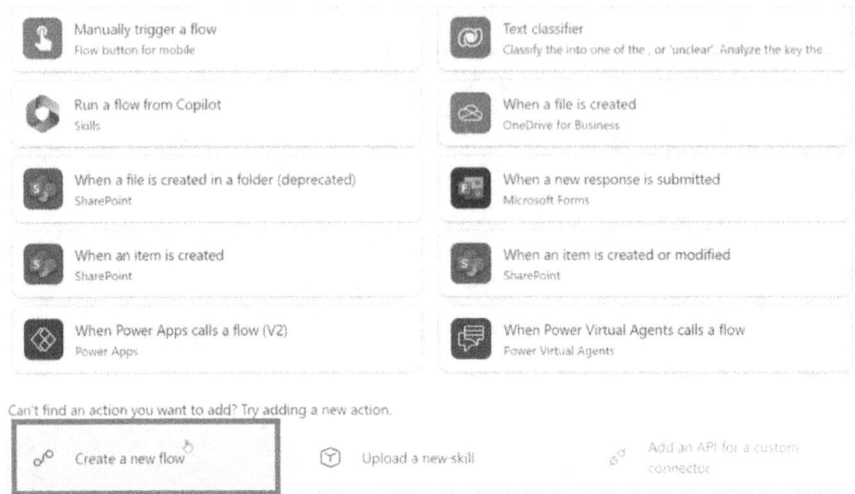

Figure 6-12. *Create new flow*

This takes you to the Power Automate screen. You must provide input parameters as needed, as shown in Figure 6-13.

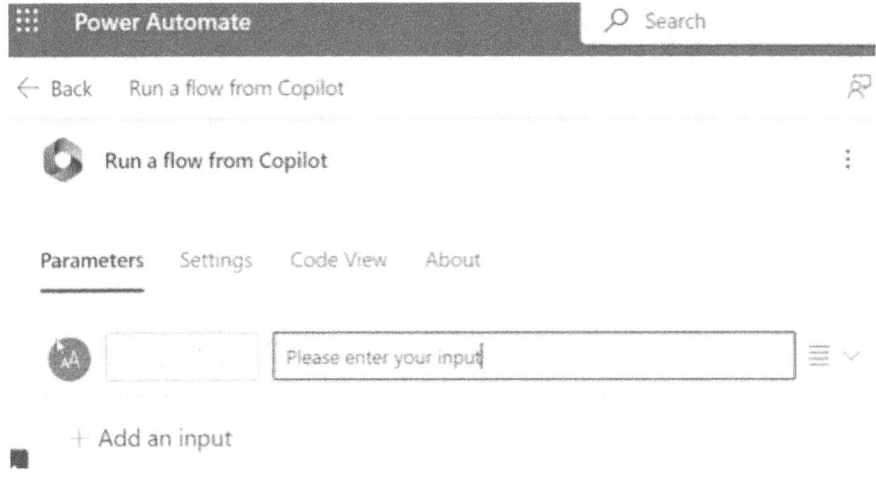

Figure 6-13. *Input parameters: Power Automate flow*

CHAPTER 6   DEPLOYING, MONITORING, AND ENSURING AI SAFETY

For the question you entered in the input parameter, you can create an action to make an HTTP request, as shown in Figure 6-14. You have to enter information like URL, method, header, and so forth.

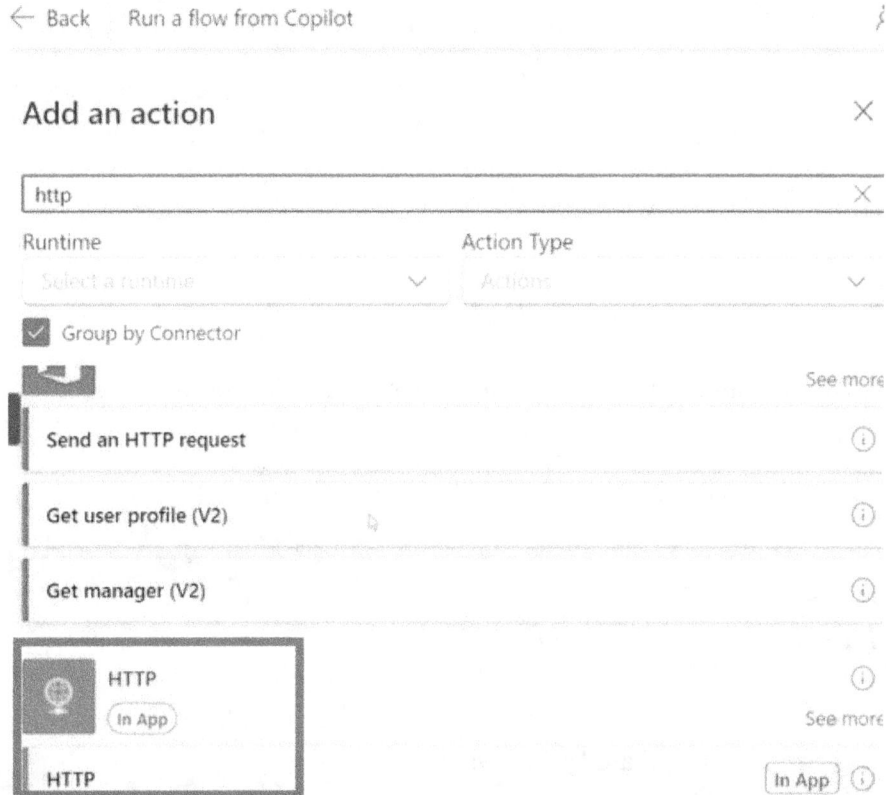

Figure 6-14. *HTTP request*

The next step is to add the output of your copilot as shown in Figure 6-15.

149

CHAPTER 6   DEPLOYING, MONITORING, AND ENSURING AI SAFETY

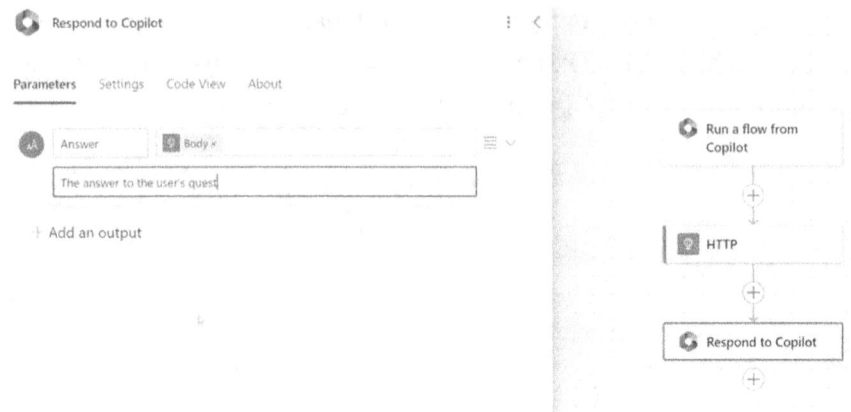

Figure 6-15. *Add copilot output*

Save a draft of your workflow and click the **Publish** button (see Figure 6-16).

Figure 6-16. *Save draft and publish*

Now go to the Copilot Studio and refresh. You should be able to see the new workflow you created as shown in Figure 6-17.

CHAPTER 6   DEPLOYING, MONITORING, AND ENSURING AI SAFETY

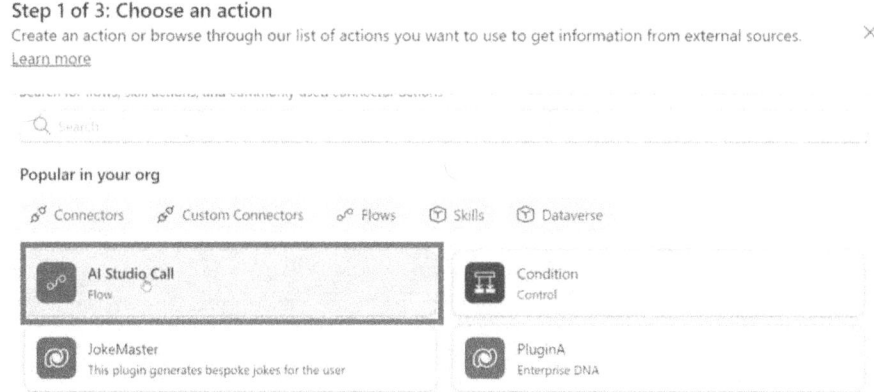

Figure 6-17. Flow in Copilot Studio

In step 2, review the inputs and outputs, which were configured while creating the flow as highlighted in Figure 6-18.

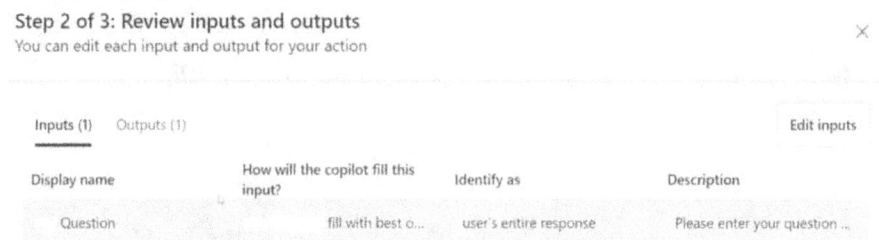

Figure 6-18. Review input and output

The final step is to review and finish as shown in Figure 6-19. Here, you can review all the information and click the **Finish** button.

151

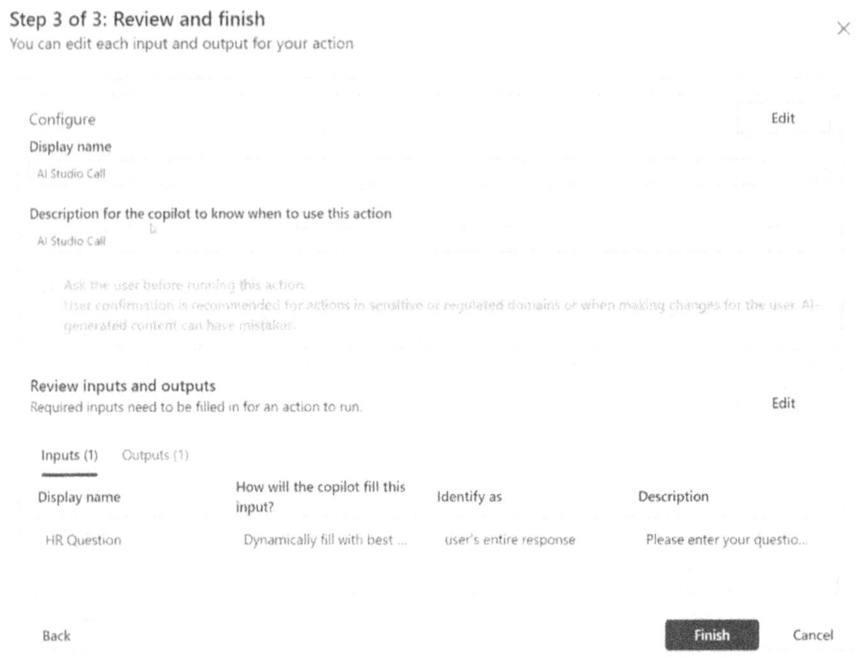

CHAPTER 6   DEPLOYING, MONITORING, AND ENSURING AI SAFETY

Step 3 of 3: Review and finish
You can edit each input and output for your action

Configure   Edit
Display name
AI Studio Call

Description for the copilot to know when to use this action
AI Studio Call

Ask the user before running this action.
User confirmation is recommended for actions in sensitive or regulated domains or when making changes for the user. AI-generated content can have mistakes.

Review inputs and outputs
Required inputs need to be filled in for an action to run.   Edit

Inputs (1)   Outputs (1)

Display name	How will the copilot fill this input?	Identify as	Description
HR Question	Dynamically fill with best ...	user's entire response	Please enter your questio...

Back   Finish   Cancel

Figure 6-19. *Review and finish integration with copilot*

CHAPTER 6 DEPLOYING, MONITORING, AND ENSURING AI SAFETY

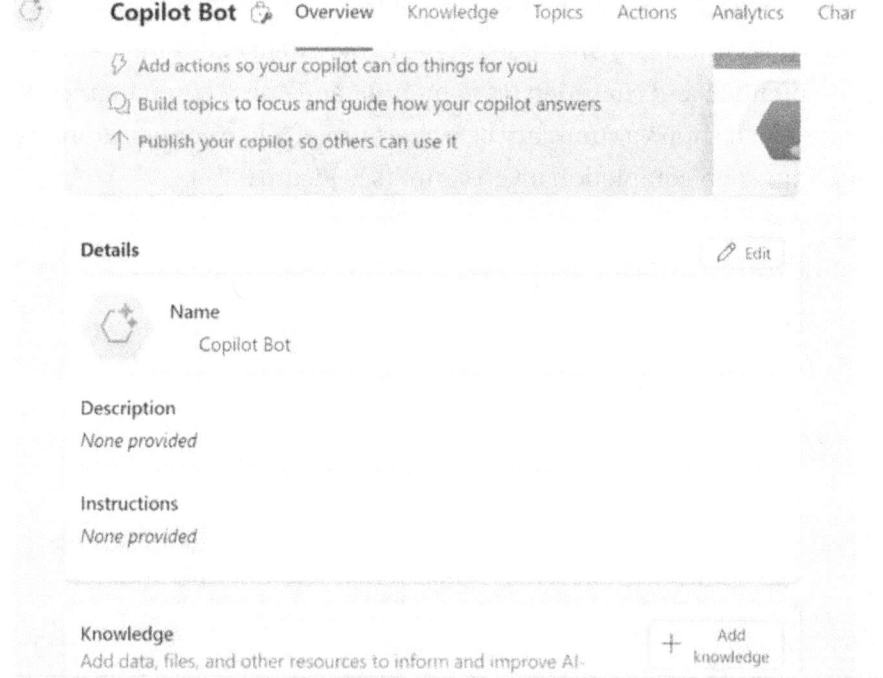

Figure 6-20. *Copilot actions setup*

As you can see in Figure 6-20, an action has been successfully set up for your copilot bot in Copilot Studio. You can use it by asking prompts or input questions.

Monitoring and Managing AI Endpoints

In the previous section, you did deployments and created endpoints. This section explores how you can effectively monitor and manage endpoints in AI Foundry. Point to note here is that endpoints are up and running 24/7. So, it also gets charged when they are up and running. So, monitoring the endpoints to reduce/save costs is good.

CHAPTER 6   DEPLOYING, MONITORING, AND ENSURING AI SAFETY

To monitor the deployment and endpoints, go to the home page of AI Foundry, click the deployment, select the deployment endpoint that you want to monitor, and click **Metrics** to monitor and check common metrics information. It shows a summary of requests, total token counts, prompts token count, and completion token count (see Figure 6-21).

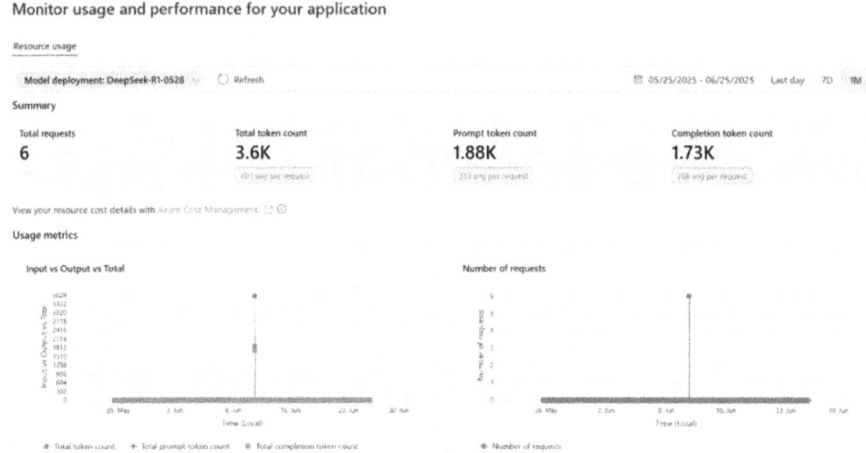

Figure 6-21. *Monitor usage of AI Foundry deployment endpoints*

If you want to know more about cost-related metrics, use the Azure cost management deep link. Metrics is an analysis tool in the Azure portal that allows you to monitor and analyze metrics of your Azure resources. Go to your Azure portal, select **Monitor** in the search box, and select **Metrics** from the left navigation bar. You can also enable various filters based on scope, resource type, and so forth, as highlighted in Figure 6-22.

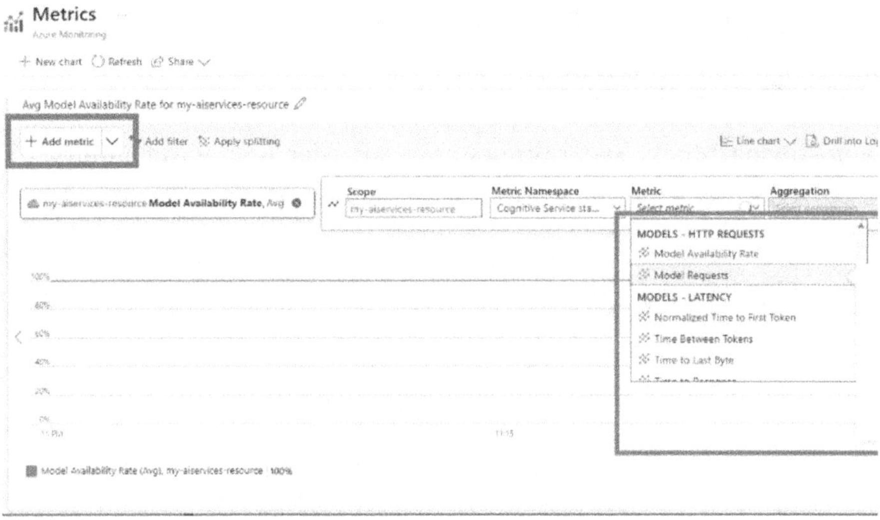

CHAPTER 6   DEPLOYING, MONITORING, AND ENSURING AI SAFETY

Figure 6-22. *Metrics in the Azure portal*

If you no longer need the deployment endpoint, then you can also delete the deployment. Go to the deployment overview page and click **Delete deployment**, as highlighted in Figure 6-23. You get a pop-up box to confirm the deletion of the deployment as well as the endpoint. Once you click it, the deployment endpoint is deleted.

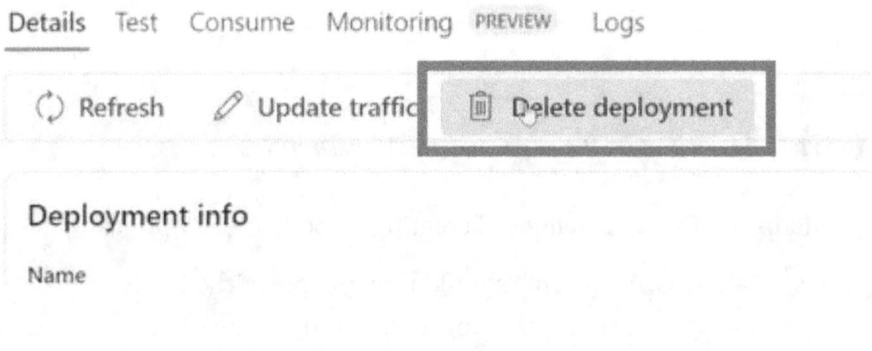

Figure 6-23. *Delete deployment*

155

CHAPTER 6 DEPLOYING, MONITORING, AND ENSURING AI SAFETY

Security, Governance, and AI Trustworthiness

Before diving into the security and governance features of AI Foundry, let's first discuss Microsoft's responsible AI standards, as illustrated in Figure 6-24.

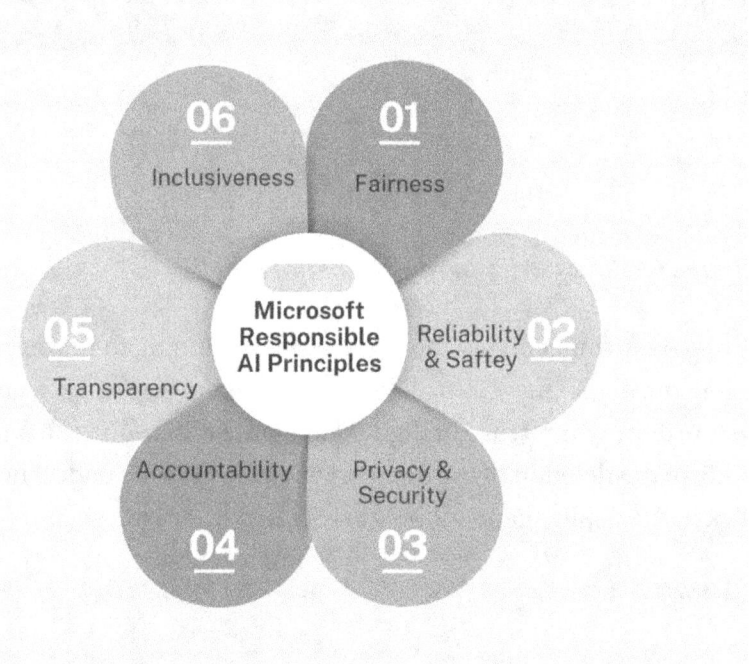

Figure 6-24. *Microsoft's responsible AI principles*

Microsoft has six principles of creating responsible AI applications.

- **Fairness**: AI systems should treat people fairly. It should ensure quality of service and resource availability based on region, culture, and demographics.

156

- **Reliability and safety**: AI systems should be developed in line with the design ideas and values to avoid creating harm.

- **Privacy and security**: Regulatory frameworks mandate organizations to follow privacy principles while processing personal information. If your machine learning model is using any third-party tool or package, even without access to the training data, it can still cause leakage of sensitive personal information.

- **Accountability**: The organizations and individuals are responsible for designing, developing, and deploying AI applications, ensuring they operate ethically and transparently. It emphasizes supporting AI models in making decisions but let's humans remain answerable for the outcomes.

- **Transparency**: Users and business people must be able to see how the service works and validate the functionality end-to-end. Increased transparency helps AI consumers to better understand the AI model.

- **Inclusiveness**: Inclusiveness means designing and implementing AI systems that are accessible, usable, and beneficial for a wide range of people regardless of their background and abilities.

Azure AI Content Safety is an AI service that detects harmful user and AI-generated content in applications and services. It enables you to detect and prevent harmful output content of your AI application. From the AI Foundry portal, you can check interactive content safety, which allows you to view, explore, and try sample code to detect harmful content across various modalities. You can use Azure Content Safety for the following scenarios.

- Text
  - Moderate text content to identify and categorize based on the different security levels.
  - Groundness detection to validate if AI responses are based on trusted and user-provided sources.
  - Prompt Shields provides a unified API to address jailbreak and indirect attacks.

- Image
  - Moderate image content filters and assesses image content and detect harmful visuals.
  - Handle a combination of images and text to assess overall context and potential risks across multiple types.

- Custom categories
  - Enable users to define categories to filter content based on their needs and scenarios.
  - Set up safety system messages to instruct AI on desired behavior and limitations to prevent unwanted outputs.

Content filtering in AI Foundry works with core and image generation models. It is powered by Azure Content Safety. Let's discuss how to create a content filter in AI Foundry.

The first step is to go to the AI Foundry portal and navigate to your project. Go to the **Guardrails + controls** in the left pane and select **Content filters**, as shown in Figure 6-25.

CHAPTER 6 DEPLOYING, MONITORING, AND ENSURING AI SAFETY

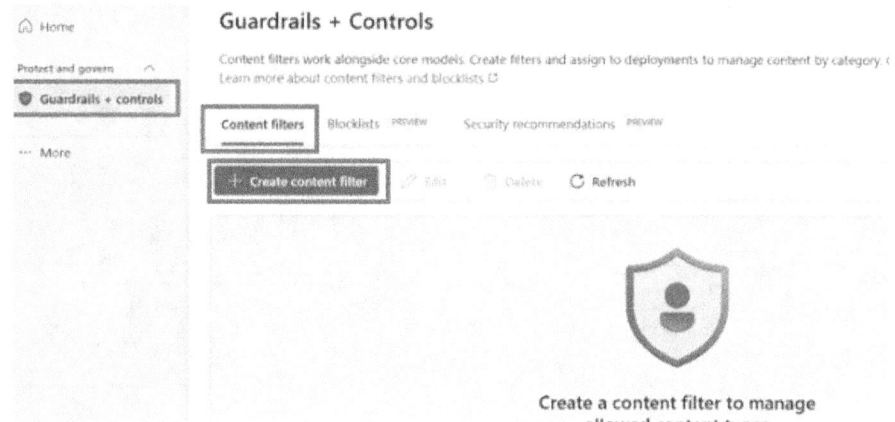

Figure 6-25. Create content filter in AI Foundry

Then, select **Create content filter** and enter basic information, as highlighted in Figure 6-26.

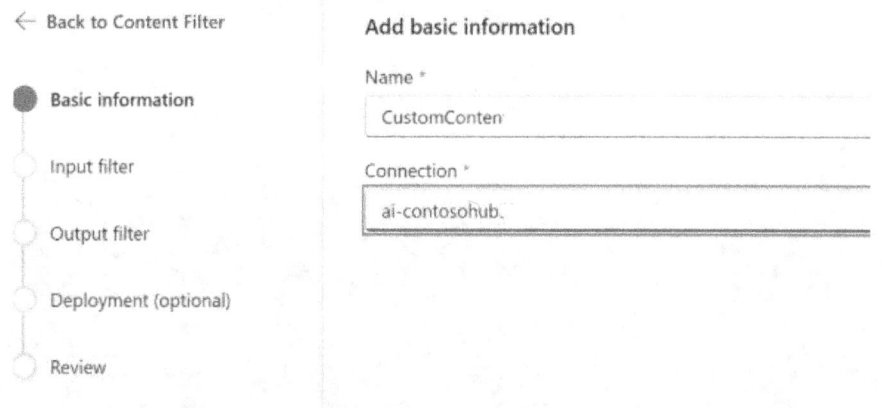

Figure 6-26. Basic information to create filters

The next step is to create input filters per your needs, as highlighted in Figure 6-27.

CHAPTER 6 DEPLOYING, MONITORING, AND ENSURING AI SAFETY

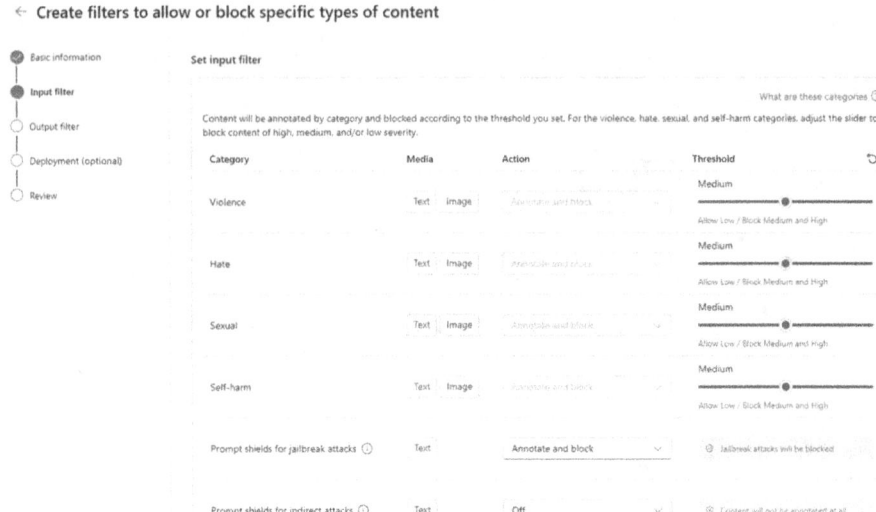

Figure 6-27. Input filter to create content

Next, configure output filters as highlighted in Figure 6-28.

Figure 6-28. Configure output filters to create content filter

CHAPTER 6   DEPLOYING, MONITORING, AND ENSURING AI SAFETY

Optionally, if you want to deploy the content filter, then you can associate the content filter with a specific deployment, as highlighted in Figure 6-29.

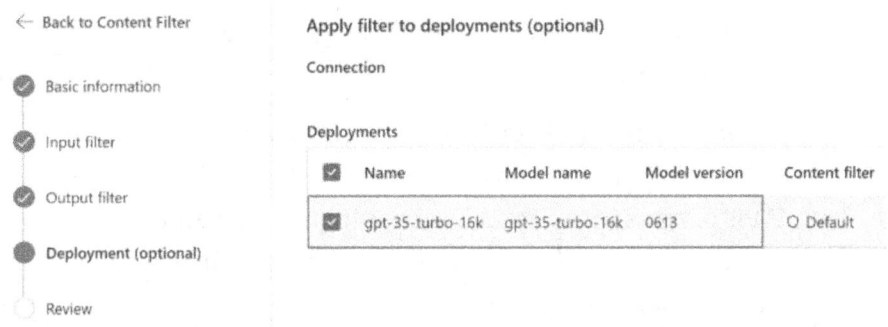

Figure 6-29. Content filter deployment

You can implement role-based access control in AI Foundry to manage authentication efficiently. AI Foundry has the following roles available.

- **Azure AI user**: Read access to all AI projects

- **Azure AI project manager**: The user can perform management actions in the AI Foundry project to build, develop, and grant conditional access.

- **Azure AI account owner**: Full access to manage Azure AI Projects

You can use a private link to secure communication with your AI Foundry project. Azure AI Foundry supports keyless authentication and customer-managed keys to keep your data secure.

161

Users may face these common challenges when deploying prompt flows, RAG pipelines, or integrated AI services.

- **Model/environment configuration errors**: Mismatch between selected model capabilities and actual prompt requirements. To fix this, use model catalogs to validate token limits, modality support, and latency expectations.

- **Dependency conflicts**: In a prompt flow, library version mismatches may occur if you call external APIs or run scripts. To fix, use requirements.txt and Azure-hosted environments wisely. Test flows in dev environments before deployment.

- **Endpoint failures**: Deployed endpoints may intermittently fail or timeout. To fix, ensure you're using retries, proper error handling, and monitoring in production-grade flows.

- **Data access/index issues** (in RAG setups): Retrieval-augmented generation (RAG) flows may fail if the index or data source is missing or misconfigured. To fix, confirm data ingestion and index creation steps are successful; check security roles for access permissions.

- **Prompt flow output inconsistency**: Slight model changes or input variations may cause unexpected output behaviors. To fix, validate output ranges with prompt testing, and implement fallback strategies.

Having a clear disaster recovery strategy plan is necessary for your AI Foundry solution.

- Backup and replication
- Cross-region deployment

CHAPTER 6   DEPLOYING, MONITORING, AND ENSURING AI SAFETY

- Automated redeployment scripts
- Monitoring and alerting
- Business continuity playbook

Conclusion

As this final chapter concludes—and your journey through *Level Up with Azure AI Foundry*—you now stand equipped with theoretical knowledge and the practical skills needed to bring generative AI to life in real-world applications.

You explored how to deploy and debug prompt flows, ensuring your solutions are production-ready and resilient. From there, you moved into consuming AI Foundry endpoints within diverse applications, bridging the gap between experimentation and tangible business impact. The chapter then took a step further, illustrating how to integrate AI Foundry with Microsoft Copilot, enabling richer, more intelligent user experiences. Finally, you learned the importance of monitoring and managing AI endpoints, reinforcing the ongoing responsibility of maintaining performance, compliance, and responsible AI practices.

Bringing AI into production isn't the finish line—it's the beginning of transformation. With the Azure AI Foundry, you've learned how to build, refine, and deliver AI-powered solutions with confidence and accountability. Whether creating internal tools, customer-facing experiences, or next-generation copilots, you now have the architecture, tools, and mindset to drive innovation responsibly and at scale.

Let this book be your launchpad. Keep exploring, keep experimenting, and most importantly—keep leveling up.

Index

A, B

AI-driven applications, 1
Azure AI Document
       Intelligence, 126
    cloud-based AI service, 122
    create prompt flow, 126, 127
    design prompt, 127
    run flow, 128
    setup, 122, 123
    test, 125
    upload sample invoices, 123, 125
Azure AI Foundry
    architecture, 13
    components, 9
    connections, 20, 22
    GPT model, 11
    hub, 17–19, 32
        OpenAI model, 33, 34
        use/connect OpenAI, 34–36
    management center, 15, 16
    multimodal GenAI
        applications, 11
    OpenAI, 14, 15
    project, 19
    services, 10
    setting up environment,
        24–29, 31, 32

Azure AI Search, 95
Azure AI Speech, 12
Azure Cosmos DB, 12
Azure OpenAI,
    14, 22, 23, 32, 57
Azure Speech Studio, 110–117

C, D

Chain-of-thought (CoT)
    prompting, 8
Chatbot, 44
ChatGPT, 2
Chat playground
    add data, 51
    AI Foundry SDK, 49, 50
    deploy model, 45
    LLM models, 47
    manual evaluation, 49
    parameters, 46
    permissions, 44
    variety, 48
Cross-origin resource sharing
    (CORS), 124

E

Embedding, 7

INDEX

F
Few-shot prompting, 8

G, H, I, J
GenAI-based applications, 23
Generative AI
    ChatGPT, 2, 3
    data science, 3
    embedding, 7
    LLMs, 5, 6
    machine learning, 4
    prompt engineering, 6, 7
    technologies/use cases, 5

K
Knowledge base, 92

L
Large language model operations (LLMOps), 60
Large language models (LLMs), 5, 41, 60, 89, 107

M
Machine learning operations (MLOps), 60
Microsoft Copilot, 71, 145–153, 163
Model as a service (MaaS), 43
Model benchmarks, 41–43
Model catalogs, 36–38, 40, 41
Model deployments, 43, 44
Multimodal AI capabilities
    AI vision image analysis, 117–121
    Azure AI Document Intelligence, 122
    Microsoft's AI portfolio, 109, 110
    single-model AI, 108

N
Natural language processing (NLP), 129

O
Optical character recognition (OCR), 96, 118

P, Q
Personally Identifiable Information (PII), 128–131
Prompt catalogs
    features, 53
    instructions, 51
    practices, 54, 56
    techniques, 52
Prompt chaining, 9
Prompt engineering, 6–9
Prompt flow
    Copilot stack, 71–73
    creating I/O flows, 62–71
    deploying/debugging

INDEX

AI Foundry deployment
  options, 134, 135
  custom evaluation, 137, 138
  evaluation method, 140
  managed compute, 142
  model catalog, 141
  upload dataset, 139
features, 61
function calling, 86, 87
integrating external APIs, 83, 84, 86
lifecycle, 60, 61
structured AI workflows, 59
web classification
  compute session, 78, 79
  connection, 74–77
  development, 77
  execution, 80–83
  setup LLM node, 79, 80

R

Retrieval-augmented generation (RAG), 107
  connecting/manage data sources, 102, 103, 105
  GPT, 90
  LLMs, 90, 92–94
  prompt flow
    architecture, 95
    Azure AI Search, 95, 96
    create project, 99, 101, 102
    setup infrastructure, 97, 98

S, T, U, V, W, X, Y

Safety
  monitor and manage endpoints, 153–155
Security and governance
  AI standards, 156
  Azure Content Safety, 157
  create content filter, 159–161
  integrated AI services, 162, 163
  principles, 156, 157
Small language models (SLMs), 41
Software development kit (SDK), 61
Speech synthesis, 113
Speech Synthesis Markup Language (SSML), 110
Standard operating procedures (SOPs), 90

Z

Zero-shot prompting, 8, 52

GPSR Compliance
The European Union's (EU) General Product Safety Regulation (GPSR) is a set of rules that requires consumer products to be safe and our obligations to ensure this.

If you have any concerns about our products, you can contact us on

ProductSafety@springernature.com

In case Publisher is established outside the EU, the EU authorized representative is:

Springer Nature Customer Service Center GmbH
Europaplatz 3
69115 Heidelberg, Germany

www.ingramcontent.com/pod-product-compliance
Lightning Source LLC
LaVergne TN
LVHW021958060526
838201LV00048B/1615